KITCHEN LIBRARY
Entrées

KITCHEN LIBRARY
Entrées

JANE PRICE

MURDOCH BOOKS

contents

Classic and Contemporary Favorites

When it comes to cooking an entrée course, there are limitless possibilities. What you choose depends on a few considerations, such as the occasion, the season, and also a guest's dietary needs. Often the decision of what to cook is complicated by cookbooks themselves – few are actually devoted exclusively to the entrée course and the cook must consult a range of books to find just the right recipe. *Kitchen Library Entrées* brings together the entire spectrum of entrée course dishes, making choosing painless. From laid-back family meals to the most elegant of offerings, all the favorites are here.

There's endless inspiration for entertaining. Seafood, for example, suggests luxury, whether in the form of seared scallops, a whole baked fish, or a complex stew like bouillabaisse. Refined meat dishes, like rabbit with rosemary and red wine, or herbed rack of veal, will similarly satisfy the most discerning of palates and look impressive too. When the occasion calls for a more relaxed approach, there are dozens of ideas. Barbecued food is the quintessential relaxed fare and, when fine weather allows for al fresco dining, there's nothing more delicious than the aromas of skewers, steaks, or cutlets as they sizzle over an open flame.

Beyond entertaining and special occasions, there's the inescapable routine of providing family meals – without fresh ideas cooking every night can become a chore. From classic to contemporary, from fast to fussy, and from the very familiar to the exoticism of foreign cuisines, the recipes in *Kitchen Library Entrées* will supply a recipe for any occasion.

seafood

Seafood, Fennel and Potato Stew

🌿 SERVES 6

🌿 PREPARATION TIME: 25 MINUTES

🌿 COOKING TIME: 30 MINUTES

18–20 black mussels
6 baby octopus
16 raw shrimp
1 large fennel bulb
2 tablespoons olive oil
2 leeks, white part only, thinly sliced
2 garlic cloves, crushed
1/2 teaspoon paprika
2 tablespoons Pernod or Ricard (see Notes)
2/3 cup dry white wine
1/4 teaspoon saffron threads
1/4 teaspoon thyme
1 lb 2 oz fish cutlets (such as swordfish),
   cut into 6 large chunks
14 oz small boiling potatoes (see Notes)

Scrub the mussels with a stiff brush and pull out the hairy beards. Discard any broken mussels or open ones that don't close when tapped on the bench. Rinse well.

Use a small, sharp knife to cut off the octopus heads. Grasp the bodies and push the beaks out with your index finger. Remove and discard. Slit the heads and remove the gut, then wash well.

Peel the shrimp, leaving the tails intact. Gently pull out the dark vein from each shrimp back, starting at the head end.

Remove the fennel fronds and reserve. Trim off any discolored parts of the fennel and thinly slice. Heat the oil in a large frying pan over medium heat. Add the fennel, leek, and garlic. Stir in the paprika, season lightly, and cook for 8 minutes, or until softened. Add the Pernod or Ricard and wine, and boil for 1 minute, or until reduced by one-third.

Add the mussels to the pan, cover and cook, shaking the pan occasionally for 4–5 minutes, discarding any mussels that haven't opened after that time. Remove from the pan and allow to cool. Remove the mussel meat from the shells and set aside.

Add the saffron and thyme to the pan and cook, stirring over medium heat, for 1–2 minutes. Season if necessary, then transfer to a large, flameproof casserole dish.

Stir the octopus, shrimp, fish, and potatoes into the stew. Cover and cook gently for 10 minutes, or until the potatoes and seafood are tender. Add the mussels, cover and heat through. Garnish with the reserved fennel fronds and serve.

NOTES: Pernod and Ricard are aniseed-flavored liqueurs that complement the fennel.
   Choose very small potatoes for this recipe. Otherwise, cut larger ones in half.

Sole with Shrimp and Creamy Dill Sauce

❧ SERVES 4
❧ PREPARATION TIME: 15 MINUTES
❧ COOKING TIME: 20 MINUTES

12 raw large shrimp
2½ cups fish stock
1½ tablespoons butter
1 garlic clove, finely chopped
2 tablespoons all-purpose flour
2 tablespoons whipping cream
olive oil, for pan-frying
4 x 7 oz sole fillets
1 tablespoon snipped chives
1 tablespoon chopped dill
chives or dill sprigs, to garnish

Peel the shrimp, leaving the tails intact. Gently pull out the dark vein from each shrimp back, starting from the head end. Heat the stock in a saucepan and bring to a boil. Reduce the heat and simmer for 10 minutes, or until the liquid has reduced. You will need 1½ cups fish stock.

Melt the butter in a small saucepan and add the garlic. Stir in the flour and cook for 1 minute, or until pale and foaming. Remove from the heat and gradually stir in the stock. Return to the heat and stir constantly until the sauce boils and thickens. Reduce the heat and simmer for 1 minute. Remove from the heat and stir in the cream. Season to taste. Keep warm.

Heat a little oil in a frying pan and cook the fish fillets over medium heat for 2 minutes each side, or until the fish flakes easily when tested with a fork. Transfer to serving plates. Add the shrimp to the same pan and cook for 2–3 minutes. Stir the chives and dill into the sauce, arrange the shrimp and spoon the sauce over the top. Garnish with chives or dill.

Tuna with Sorrel Hollandaise

❧ SERVES 4
❧ PREPARATION TIME: 15 MINUTES
❧ COOKING TIME: 10 MINUTES

SORREL HOLLANDAISE
15 young sorrel leaves, stems removed
⅔ cup butter
3 egg yolks
1 tablespoon lemon juice

4 x 5½ oz tuna steaks
2 tablespoons olive oil

To make the sorrel hollandaise, put the sorrel leaves in a bowl, cover with boiling water, drain and rinse in cold water. Pat the leaves dry with paper towels and chop roughly. Melt the butter in a small saucepan. Put the egg yolks in a food processor and process for 20 seconds. With the motor running, add the hot butter in a thin, steady stream and process until thick and creamy. Add the lemon juice and sorrel and season to taste. Process for another 20 seconds.

Brush the tuna with the oil. Heat a large frying pan and cook the tuna for 2–3 minutes each side over medium heat. Spoon the sorrel hollandaise over the tuna and serve.

Sole with Shrimp and Creamy Dill Sauce

Caponata with Tuna

❀ SERVES 6
❀ PREPARATION TIME: 25 MINUTES
❀ COOKING TIME: 45 MINUTES

CAPONATA
1 lb 10 oz eggplant, cut into 1/2 inch cubes
1/2 cup olive oil
1 onion, chopped
3 celery stalks, chopped
1 lb 2 oz ripe tomatoes, peeled, and cut
   into 1/2 inch cubes
2 tablespoons capers, rinsed, and squeezed
   dry
2/3 cup green olives, pitted
1 tablespoon sugar
1/2 cup red wine vinegar

6 x 7 oz tuna steaks
olive oil, for brushing

Sprinkle the eggplant with salt and leave in a colander for 1 hour. Rinse under cold water and pat dry. Heat 2 tablespoons of the oil in a frying pan over medium heat and cook half the eggplant for 4–5 minutes, or until golden and soft. Remove from the pan and drain on crumpled paper towels. Repeat with another 2 tablespoons of the oil and the remaining eggplant.

Heat the remaining olive oil in the same pan, add the onion and celery, and cook for 5–6 minutes, or until softened. Reduce the heat to low, add the tomato and simmer for 15 minutes. Stir in the capers, olives, sugar, and vinegar, season and continue to simmer for 10 minutes, or until slightly reduced. Stir in the eggplant. Remove from the heat and cool.

Heat a chargrill plate and brush lightly with olive oil. Cook the tuna for 2–3 minutes each side, or to your liking. Serve with the caponata.

Pan-Fried Salmon with Gremolata

❀ SERVES 4
❀ PREPARATION TIME: 10 MINUTES
❀ COOKING TIME: 10 MINUTES

GREMOLATA
4 tablespoons finely chopped Italian
   parsley
2 teaspoons grated lemon zest
2 teaspoons grated orange zest
2 garlic cloves, crushed
3 teaspoons capers, rinsed, and squeezed
   dry

1 1/2 tablespoons butter
1 tablespoon olive oil
4 x 7 oz salmon fillets

To make the gremolata, combine the parsley, lemon zest, orange zest, and garlic in a small bowl with the capers. Mix well and set aside.

Heat a large frying pan and add the butter and olive oil. Add the salmon fillets and pan-fry over high heat on both sides for about 2–3 minutes each side, or until cooked as desired. Serve the salmon topped with the gremolata.

Caponata with Tuna

Baked Fish with Noodle Filling

❧ SERVES 10–12
❧ PREPARATION TIME: 20 MINUTES
❧ COOKING TIME: 50 MINUTES

4 lb 8 oz ocean trout or 1 whole salmon,
   boned and butterflied (see Note)
3 1/2 oz thin rice noodles
1 tablespoon peanut oil
6 red Asian shallots, chopped
2 red chilies, chopped
2 tablespoons grated fresh ginger
3/4 cup canned water chestnuts, chopped
3/4 cup canned bamboo shoots, chopped
6 scallions, sliced
2 tablespoons chopped cilantro stem
3 tablespoons chopped cilantro leaves
2 tablespoons fish sauce
2 tablespoons grated jaggery or unpacked
   brown sugar

LIME BUTTER SAUCE
4 kaffir lime leaves, finely shredded
2 tablespoons lime juice
1/2 cup butter

Preheat the oven to 350°F. Pat the fish dry and use tweezers to remove any remaining small bones.

Soak the noodles in boiling water for 10 minutes. Drain well, pat dry, and cut into short lengths.

Heat the oil in a frying pan and cook the shallots, chili, and ginger over medium heat for about 5 minutes, or until the shallots are golden. Transfer to a bowl. Add the noodles, water chestnuts, bamboo shoots, scallion, cilantro stem and leaves, fish sauce, and jaggery to the bowl and mix well.

Open the trout or salmon out flat and spread the noodle filling over the center. Fold the fish over to enclose the filling and secure with string every 2 inches along the fish. Place onto a baking sheet lined with foil and bake for 30–40 minutes, or until tender.

To make the sauce, put the kaffir lime leaves, lime juice, and butter in a saucepan and cook over medium heat until the butter turns nutty brown.

Cut the salmon into slices, discarding the string, then serve topped with the sauce.

NOTE: A fish that has been butterflied has been carefully slit through the middle, along the bones, but not all the way through. The effect is of having a hinge on one side of the fish. Another term for this is 'pocket boning'. Ask your fishmonger to do this for you.

Steamed Fish with Ginger and Chili

❀ SERVES 4
❀ PREPARATION TIME: 15 MINUTES
❀ COOKING TIME: 10 MINUTES

4 x 7 oz skinless firm white fish fillets
2 inch piece ginger, cut into fine shreds
2 medium garlic cloves, chopped
2 teaspoons chopped red chili
2 tablespoons finely chopped cilantro
    stems
3 medium scallions, cut into fine shreds
    1½ inches long
2 tablespoons lime juice
lime wedges, to serve

Line a bamboo steaming basket with banana leaves or parchment paper (this is so the fish will not stick or taste of bamboo).

Arrange the fish in the basket and top with the ginger, garlic, chili and cilantro. Cover and steam over a wok or large saucepan of boiling water for 5–6 minutes.

Remove the lid and sprinkle the scallions and lime juice over the fish. Cover and steam for 30 seconds, or until the fish is cooked. Serve immediately with wedges of lime and steamed rice.

Grilled Fish with Fennel and Lemon

❀ SERVES 4
❀ PREPARATION TIME: 10 MINUTES
❀ COOKING TIME: 10 MINUTES

4 whole red mullet or bream, cleaned,
    scaled and gutted
1 medium lemon, thinly sliced
1 baby fennel bulb, thinly sliced
1½ tablespoons fennel seeds
¼ cup lemon juice
⅓ cup olive oil

Cut three diagonal slashes on both sides of each fish. Put two or three slices of lemon and some slices of fennel bulb in the cavity of each fish. Bruise the fennel seeds roughly, using a mortar and pestle. Sprinkle both sides of each fish with the cracked fennel seeds and some salt and rub well into the flesh.

Mix the lemon juice and olive oil in a bowl. Heat a chargrill pan or plate and when very hot, add the fish. Drizzle a little of the juice and oil over each fish. After 5 minutes, turn carefully with tongs, ensuring the filling doesn't fall out, and drizzle with the oil mix. Gently flake a piece of flesh with a fork to test whether it is cooked through, then serve with salad.

Steamed Fish Cutlets with Ginger and Chili

Seafood Stew (Zarzuela)

✻ SERVES 4

✻ PREPARATION TIME: 40 MINUTES

✻ COOKING TIME: 1 HOUR 10 MINUTES

1 x 14 oz raw lobster tail
12–15 black mussels
3½ cups diced skinless firm white fish
  fillets
all-purpose flour, seasoned
2–3 tablespoons olive oil
¾ cup squid rings
12 large raw shrimp
½ cup white wine
½ cup brandy
3 tablespoons chopped parsley,
  to garnish

SOFRITO SAUCE
2 large tomatoes
1 tablespoon olive oil
2 medium onions, finely chopped
1 tablespoon concentrated tomato purée

PICADA SAUCE
3 slices white bread, crusts removed
1 tablespoon toasted almonds
3 medium garlic cloves
1 tablespoon olive oil

To make the sofrito sauce, score a cross in the base of each tomato. Put in a heatproof bowl and cover with boiling water. Leave for 30 seconds, transfer to cold water and peel the skin away from the cross. Cut the tomatoes in half, scoop out the seeds and chop the flesh.

Heat the oil in a saucepan over medium heat. Add the onion and stir for 5 minutes without browning. Add the tomato, tomato purée and ½ cup water and stir over medium heat for 10 minutes. Stir in another ½ cup water, season and set aside.

To make the picada sauce, finely chop the bread, almonds and garlic in a food processor. With the motor running, gradually add the oil to form a paste, adding another ½ tablespoon of oil if necessary.

Preheat the oven to 350°F. Cut the lobster tail into rounds through the membrane that separates the shell segments and set aside. Scrub the mussels with a stiff brush and pull out the hairy beards. Discard any broken mussels, or open ones that don't close when tapped on the bench. Rinse well.

Lightly coat the fish in flour. Heat the oil in a large frying pan and fry the fish in batches over medium heat for 2–3 minutes, or until cooked and golden brown all over. Transfer to a large casserole dish. Add a little oil to the pan if necessary, add the squid and cook, stirring, for 1–2 minutes. Remove and add to the fish. Cook the lobster rounds and shrimp for 2–3 minutes, or until the shrimp turn pink, then add to the soup.

Add the wine to the pan and bring to a boil. Reduce the heat, add the mussels, cover and steam for 4–5 minutes. Add to the soup, discarding any unopened mussels. Pour the brandy into one side of the pan and, when it has warmed, carefully ignite the brandy. Gently shake the pan until the flames die down. Pour over the seafood in the casserole dish. Pour the sofrito sauce over the top. Cover and bake for 20 minutes. Stir in the picada sauce and cook for a further 10 minutes, or until warmed through. Sprinkle with parsley and serve.

Baked Fish with Tomato and Onion

※ SERVES 4
※ PREPARATION TIME: 20 MINUTES
※ COOKING TIME: 45 MINUTES

¼ cup olive oil
2 medium onions, finely chopped
1 small celery stalk, finely chopped
1 small carrot, finely chopped
2 medium garlic cloves, chopped
1⅔ cups canned chopped tomatoes
2 tablespoons puréed tomatoes
¼ teaspoon dried oregano
½ teaspoon sugar
1¾ oz white bread, preferably one-day old
1 lb 2 oz skinless firm white fish fillets
3 tablespoons chopped Italian parsley
1 tablespoon lemon juice

Preheat the oven to 350°F. Heat 2 tablespoons of the oil in a heavy-based frying pan. Add the onion, celery and carrot and cook over low heat for 10 minutes, or until soft. Add the garlic, cook for 2 minutes, then add the chopped tomato, puréed tomato, oregano and sugar. Simmer for about 10 minutes, stirring occasionally, until reduced and thickened. Season.

To make the breadcrumbs, chop the bread in a food processor for a few minutes, until fine crumbs form.

Arrange the fish in a single layer in an ovenproof dish. Stir the chopped parsley and the lemon juice into the sauce. Season to taste, and pour over the fish. Scatter the breadcrumbs all over the top and drizzle with the remaining oil. Bake for 20 minutes, or until the fish is just cooked.

Fish Fillets with Harissa and Olives

※ SERVES 4
※ PREPARATION TIME: 15 MINUTES
※ COOKING TIME: 25 MINUTES

⅓ cup olive oil
4 skinless firm white fish fillets
seasoned flour, for dusting
1 medium onion, chopped
2 medium garlic cloves, crushed
1⅔ cups canned chopped tomatoes
2 teaspoons harissa
2 bay leaves
1 cinnamon stick
1 cup medium Kalamata olives
1 tablespoon lemon juice
2 tablespoons chopped Italian parsley

Heat half the olive oil in a heavy-based frying pan. Dust the fish fillets with flour and cook over medium heat for 2 minutes each side, or until golden. Transfer to a plate.

Add the remaining olive oil to the pan and cook the onion and garlic for 3–4 minutes, or until softened. Add the chopped tomato, harissa, bay leaves and cinnamon. Cook for 10 minutes, or until the sauce has thickened. Season to taste.

Return the fish to the pan, add the olives and cover the fish with the sauce. Remove the bay leaves and cinnamon stick and continue cooking for 2 minutes, or until the fish is tender. Add the lemon juice and parsley and serve.

Baked Fish with Tomato and Onion

Stuffed Squid with Rice

☙ SERVES 4
☙ PREPARATION TIME: 40 MINUTES
☙ COOKING TIME: 1 HOUR 15 MINUTES

8 small squid
about 2 teaspoons all-purpose flour

STUFFING
1 small onion
2 tablespoons olive oil
2 tablespoons currants
2 tablespoons pine nuts
1/3 cup fresh breadcrumbs
1 tablespoon chopped mint
1 tablespoon chopped Italian parsley
1 egg, lightly beaten

SAUCE
1 tablespoon olive oil
1 small onion, finely chopped
1 garlic clove, crushed
1/4 cup dry white wine
1 2/3 cups canned chopped tomatoes
1/2 teaspoon sugar
1 bay leaf

RICE
5 cups fish stock
1/4 cup olive oil
1 onion, finely chopped
3 garlic cloves, crushed
1 1/4 cups calasparra or short-grain white
    rice
1/4 teaspoon cayenne pepper
3 teaspoons squid ink
1/4 cup dry white wine
1/4 cup concentrated tomato purée
2 tablespoons chopped Italian parsley

To clean the squid, pull each body from the tentacles. Cut off and keep the tentacles as well as the fins from either side of each body sac. If using the ink sacs, extract them and squeeze the ink into a small bowl. Peel the skin from each body sac and dislodge and remove the quills. Rinse under cold water.

To make the stuffing, in a food processor, finely chop the tentacles, fins, and onion. Heat the oil in a frying pan and cook the currants and pine nuts over low heat, stirring until the nuts are lightly browned. Transfer to a bowl using a slotted spoon. Add the onion mixture to the pan and cook gently over low heat for 5 minutes. Add to the bowl with the breadcrumbs, mint, parsley, and egg. Season and mix well. Stuff into the squid bodies. Close the openings and secure with toothpicks. Dust the squid with the flour.

To make the sauce, wipe out the frying pan with paper towels. Heat the oil, add the onion, and cook over low heat for 5 minutes, or until softened. Stir in the garlic, cook for 30 seconds, then add the wine. Cook over high heat for 1 minute, then add the tomato, sugar, and bay leaf. Season, reduce the heat, and simmer for 5 minutes. Stir in 1/2 cup water. Place the squid in the pan in a single layer. Simmer, covered, for about 20 minutes, or until the squid are tender.

To make the rice, bring the stock to a simmer in a saucepan. Heat the oil in a large saucepan, add the onion and cook over low heat for 5 minutes, or until softened. Add the garlic, cook for 15 seconds, then stir in the rice and cayenne pepper. Mix the ink with 1/3 cup of hot stock. Stir into the rice, then add the wine and tomato purée. Stir until the liquid has almost all evaporated, then add 1 cup of the hot stock. Simmer until this evaporates, then stir in more stock, 1 cup at a time, until the rice is tender and creamy — about 15 minutes. Cover the pan and leave off the heat for 5 minutes. Season well.

To serve, spread the rice on a warm platter and stir in the parsley. Arrange the squid on top and spoon on the sauce.

Seafood Paella

❋ SERVES 6

❋ PREPARATION TIME: 25 MINUTES

❋ COOKING TIME: 45 MINUTES

2 medium tomatoes

4 cups raw shrimp

3 cups black mussels

1¼ cups squid rings

¼ cup olive oil

1 large onion, diced

3 medium garlic cloves, finely chopped

1 small red bell pepper, seeded
and membrane removed, thinly sliced

1 small red chili, seeded and chopped,
optional

2 teaspoons paprika

1 teaspoon ground turmeric

1 tablespoon concentrated tomato purée

2 cups paella rice or risotto rice

½ cup dry white wine

¼ teaspoon saffron threads, soaked in
¼ cup hot water

5 cups fish stock

1½ cups diced skinless firm white fish
fillets

3 tablespoons chopped Italian parsley,
to serve

lemon wedges, to serve

Score a cross in the base of each tomato. Put the tomatoes in a heatproof bowl and cover with boiling water. Leave for 30 seconds, then transfer to cold water and peel the skin away from the cross. Cut each tomato in half, scoop out the seeds and finely chop the flesh.

Peel the shrimp, leaving the tails intact. Gently pull out the dark vein from the back of each shrimp, starting at the head end. Scrub the mussels with a stiff brush and pull out the hairy beards. Discard any broken mussels or open ones that don't close when tapped on the bench. Rinse well. Refrigerate the seafood (including the squid), covered, until ready to use.

Heat the oil in a paella pan or large, deep frying pan with a lid. Add the onion, garlic, pepper and chili to the pan and cook over medium heat for 2 minutes, or until the onion and pepper are soft. Add the paprika, turmeric and 1 teaspoon salt and stir-fry for 1–2 minutes, or until fragrant. Add the chopped tomato and cook for 5 minutes, or until softened. Add the concentrated tomato purée. Stir in the rice until it's well coated.

Pour in the wine and simmer until almost absorbed. Add the saffron and its soaking liquid and all the fish stock and bring to a boil. Reduce the heat and simmer for 20 minutes, or until almost all the liquid is absorbed into the rice. There is no need to stir the rice, but you may occasionally wish to fluff it up with a fork to separate the grains.

Add the mussels to the pan, poking the shells into the rice, cover and cook for 1–2 minutes over low heat. Add the shrimp and cook for 2–3 minutes. Add the fish, cover and cook for 3 minutes. Finally, add the squid rings and cook for 1–2 minutes. By this time, the mussels should have opened; discard any unopened ones. Cook for another 2–3 minutes if the seafood is not quite cooked, but avoid overcooking or it will toughen and dry out. Remove the pan from the heat, cover loosely with foil and leave to rest for 5–10 minutes. Serve with the parsley and lemon wedges.

Chu Chee Seafood Curry

❋ SERVES 4
❋ PREPARATION TIME: 20 MINUTES
❋ COOKING TIME: 20 MINUTES

1 lb 2 oz raw king shrimp
1 lb 2 oz scallops, without roe
2¼ cups canned coconut cream (do not shake)
¼ cup chu chee curry paste (see Note)
2–3 tablespoons fish sauce
2–3 tablespoons grated jaggery or unpacked brown sugar
8 kaffir lime leaves, finely shredded
2 small red chilies, thinly sliced (optional)
1 very large handful Thai basil

Peel the shrimp, leaving the tails intact. Gently pull out the dark vein from each shrimp back, starting at the head end. Remove and discard any veins, membrane, or hard white muscle from the scallops.

Lift off the thick cream from the top of the coconut cream — there should be about 1 cup of cream — and put it in a wok. Bring to a boil, then stir in the curry paste. Reduce the heat and simmer for 10 minutes, or until fragrant, and the oil begins to separate from the cream.

Stir in the seafood and remaining coconut cream and cook for 5 minutes. Add the fish sauce, jaggery, kaffir lime leaves, and chili and cook for 1 minute. Stir in half the basil and use the rest to garnish.

NOTE: Chu chee curry paste can be bought from Asian food speciality stores.

Fish Rolls

☙ SERVES 4
☙ PREPARATION TIME: 25 MINUTES
☙ COOKING TIME: 20 MINUTES

1 large ripe tomato, peeled, seeded, and
    roughly chopped
1 tablespoon drained capers, chopped
1/4 cup stuffed green olives, chopped
3 tablespoons chopped lemon thyme
1/4 cup finely grated romano cheese
2 teaspoons finely grated lemon zest
8 thin firm skinless white fish fillets (such
    as sole or snapper)
1 cup dry white wine
2 tablespoons lemon juice
3 tablespoons lemon thyme
2 bay leaves

Preheat the oven to 325°F. Put the tomato in a
small bowl and mix with the capers, olives, thyme,
cheese, lemon zest, and 1/4 teaspoon freshly ground
black pepper.

Place the fillets, skinless side up, on a flat surface.
Spread the tomato mixture evenly onto each fillet, then
roll tightly and secure with a toothpick or skewer. Place
in a single layer in a shallow casserole dish.

Pour the combined wine, lemon juice, thyme, and bay
leaves over the fish, cover and bake for 20 minutes, or
until the fish is cooked and flakes easily when tested
with a fork.

Salmon and Lemon Cannelloni

☙ SERVES 4–6
☙ PREPARATION TIME: 25 MINUTES
☙ COOKING TIME: 40 MINUTES

16 cannelloni tubes

FILLING
1 1/2 cups canned pink salmon
1 cup ricotta cheese
1 tablespoon lemon juice
1 egg yolk, lightly beaten
2 tablespoons finely chopped onion

SAUCE
1/2 cup butter
2/3 cup all-purpose flour
2 3/4 cups whole milk
1 teaspoon finely grated lemon zest
1/4 teaspoon freshly grated nutmeg

To make the filling, drain the salmon and reserve the
liquid for the sauce. Remove and discard the skin and
bones. Flake the salmon flesh and mix with the ricotta,
lemon juice, egg yolk and onion in a bowl. Season to taste.

To make the sauce, melt the butter in a saucepan over low
heat. Stir in the flour and cook for 1 minute, or until pale
and foaming. Remove from the heat and gradually stir in
the milk. Return to the heat and stir constantly until the
sauce boils and thickens. Reduce the heat and simmer for
2 minutes. Add the reserved salmon liquid, lemon zest
and nutmeg, and season to taste. Set aside to cool.

Preheat the oven to 350°F. Fill the cannelloni tubes with
filling, using a spoon or piping bag. Spread one-third of
the sauce over the bottom of a shallow ovenproof dish,
then sit the cannelloni tubes in the dish side-by-side.
Pour the remaining sauce over the top, covering all the
exposed pasta. Bake for about 30 minutes, until bubbly.

Fish Rolls

Barbecued Seafood Platter

※ SERVES 6
※ PREPARATION TIME: 40 MINUTES
※ COOKING TIME: 30 MINUTES

6 slipper lobsters
1½ tablespoons butter, melted
1 tablespoon oil
12 black mussels
12 scallops, on the shell
12 oysters
18 raw large shrimp, unpeeled

SALSA VERDE
1 tablespoon chopped preserved lemon
⅔ cup Italian parsley
1 tablespoon capers
1 tablespoon lemon juice
3 tablespoons olive oil

VINEGAR AND SHALLOT DRESSING
¼ cup white wine vinegar
4 French shallots, finely chopped
1 tablespoon chopped chervil

PICKLED GINGER AND WASABI SAUCE
1 teaspoon soy sauce
¼ cup mirin
2 tablespoons rice wine vinegar
¼ teaspoon wasabi paste
2 tablespoons finely sliced pickled ginger

SWEET BALSAMIC DRESSING
1 tablespoon olive oil
1 tablespoon honey
½ cup balsamic vinegar

THAI CILANTRO SAUCE
½ cup sweet chili sauce
1 tablespoon lime juice
2 tablespoons chopped cilantro leaves

Freeze the lobsters for 1 hour to immobilize. Cut each lobster in half with a sharp knife, then brush the flesh with the combined butter and oil. Set aside.

Scrub the mussels with a stiff brush and pull out the hairy beards. Discard any broken mussels, or open ones that don't close when tapped on the bench. Rinse well.

Pull off any vein, membrane, or hard white muscle from the scallops, leaving any roe attached. Brush the scallops with the combined butter and oil. Cook them, shell side down, on the barbecue.

Remove the oysters from the shells, then rinse the shells under cold water. Pat the shells dry and return the oysters to their shells. Cover and refrigerate all the seafood while you make the dressings.

To make the salsa verde, combine all the ingredients in a food processor and process in short bursts until chopped. Transfer to a bowl and add enough oil to moisten the mixture. Season. Serve a dollop on each scallop.

To make the vinegar and shallot dressing, whisk the vinegar, shallot, and chervil in a bowl until combined. Pour over the cooked mussels.

To make the pickled ginger and wasabi sauce, whisk all the ingredients in a bowl until combined. Spoon over the cooked oysters.

To make the sweet balsamic dressing, heat the oil in a pan, add the honey and vinegar, bring to a boil, then boil until reduced by half. Drizzle over the cooked lobters.

To make the Thai cilantro sauce, combine all the ingredients in a jug and drizzle over the cooked shrimp.

Cook the seafood on a preheated barbecue hotplate. The mussels, scallops, oysters and shrimp all take about 2–5 minutes to cook. The lobsters are cooked when the flesh turns white and starts to come away from the shell.

Seafood Lasagne

❧ SERVES 4–6
❧ PREPARATION TIME: 15 MINUTES
❧ COOKING TIME: 45 MINUTES

9 oz instant lasagne sheets
½ cup scallops
4 cups raw shrimp
1 lb 2 oz skinless firm white fish
  fillets
½ cup butter
1 leek, thinly sliced
⅔ cup all-purpose flour
2 cups whole milk
2 cups dry white wine
1 cup grated cheddar cheese
½ cup whipping cream
⅔ cup grated parmesan cheese
2 tablespoons chopped Italian parsley

Preheat the oven to 350°F. Line a greased shallow ovenproof dish (about 12 inches square) with lasagne sheets, gently breaking them to fill any gaps. Set aside.

Slice or pull off any vein, membrane or hard white muscle from the scallops, leaving any roe attached.

Peel the shrimp and gently pull out the dark vein from the back of each shrimp, starting from the head end. Chop the seafood into even-sized pieces.

Melt the butter in a large saucepan over low heat, add the leek and cook, stirring, over medium heat for 1 minute, or until starting to soften. Stir in the flour and cook for 1 minute, or until pale and foaming. Remove from the heat and gradually stir in the combined milk and wine. Return to the heat and stir constantly over medium heat until the sauce boils and thickens. Reduce the heat and simmer for 2 minutes. Add the seafood and simmer for 1 minute. Remove from the heat, stir in the cheese, then season.

Spoon half the seafood mixture over the lasagne sheets in the dish, then top with another layer of lasagne sheets. Spoon the remaining seafood mixture over the lasagne sheets, then cover with another layer of lasagne sheets.

Pour the cream over the top, then sprinkle with the combined parmesan and parsley. Bake, uncovered, for 30 minutes, or until bubbling and golden brown.

Shrimp Laksa

❀ SERVES 4–6

❀ PREPARATION TIME: 30 MINUTES

❀ COOKING TIME: 35 MINUTES

6 cups raw shrimp

1½ tablespoons coriander seeds

1 tablespoon cumin seeds

1 teaspoon ground turmeric

1 medium onion, roughly chopped

2 teaspoons roughly chopped fresh ginger

3 medium garlic cloves

3 medium lemongrass stems, white part
   only, sliced

6 candlenuts or macadamia nuts,
   roughly chopped

4–6 small red chilies, roughly chopped

2–3 teaspoons shrimp paste

4 cups chicken stock

¼ cup vegetable oil

3 cups coconut milk

4 fresh kaffir lime leaves

2½ tablespoons lime juice

2 tablespoons fish sauce

2 tablespoons grated jaggery
   or unpacked brown sugar

2½ cups dried rice vermicelli

1 cup trimmed bean sprouts

4 fried tofu puffs, cut into thin strips

3 tablespoons chopped Vietnamese mint

1 small handful cilantro leaves

lime wedges, to serve

Peel the shrimp, leaving the tails intact. Gently pull out the dark vein from the back of each shrimp, starting from the head end.

Dry-fry the coriander seeds in a small frying pan over medium heat for 1–2 minutes, or until fragrant, tossing constantly. Grind finely using a mortar and pestle or spice grinder. Repeat the process with the cumin seeds.

Put the ground coriander and cumin, turmeric, onion, ginger, garlic, lemongrass, candlenuts, chili and shrimp paste in a food processor or blender. Add about ½ cup of the stock and blend to a fine paste.

Heat a wok over low heat, add the oil and swirl to coat the base and side. Cook the paste for 3–5 minutes, stirring constantly. Pour in the remaining stock and bring to a boil, then reduce the heat and simmer for 15 minutes, or until reduced slightly. Add the coconut milk, kaffir lime leaves, lime juice, fish sauce and sugar and simmer for 5 minutes. Add the shrimp and simmer for 2 minutes, or until pink and cooked. Do not boil or cover.

Meanwhile, soak the vermicelli in boiling water for 6–7 minutes, or until soft. Drain and divide among serving bowls along with most of the sprouts. Ladle on the hot soup then top with the tofu, mint, cilantro and the remaining sprouts. Serve with lime wedges.

Bream with Tomato Cheese Crust

❊ SERVES 4
❊ PREPARATION TIME: 40 MINUTES
❊ COOKING TIME: 15 MINUTES

2 ripe medium tomatoes
1 small onion, finely chopped
1 tablespoon concentrated tomato purée
1/2 teaspoon ground cumin
1/2 teaspoon ground coriander
Tabasco sauce, to taste
1/4 teaspoon freshly ground black pepper
1 tablespoon lemon juice
1 1/3 tablespoons melted butter
4 skinless bream fillets
3/4 cup grated cheddar cheese
1/2 cup fresh breadcrumbs
lemon wedges, to serve

Score a cross in the base of each tomato. Put in a heatproof bowl and cover with boiling water. Leave for 30 seconds, then transfer to cold water and peel the skin away from the cross. Cut each tomato in half, scoop out the seeds and finely chop the flesh.

Preheat the oven to 350°F. Lightly grease a baking sheet. Put the tomato in a small bowl and mix with the onion, concentrated tomato purée, cumin, ground coriander and Tabasco.

Combine the ground pepper, lemon juice and butter in a small bowl. Put the bream fillets on the prepared sheet. Brush each fillet with the pepper mixture and top with the tomato mixture. Sprinkle with the combined cheddar and breadcrumbs and bake for 15 minutes, or until the fish is tender and flakes easily when tested with a fork. Serve with lemon wedges.

Shrimp and Okra Gumbo

※ SERVES 8
※ PREPARATION TIME: 35 MINUTES
※ COOKING TIME: 3 HOURS

2 tablespoons olive oil
1 lb 2 oz thickly sliced okra
7 oz sliced chorizo
1²⁄₃ cups diced smoked ham
¼ cup olive oil, extra
¼ cup all-purpose flour
2 medium onions, chopped
2 medium celery stalks, diced
1 medium red pepper, diced
6 medium garlic cloves, finely chopped
½ teaspoon cayenne pepper
2 teaspoons sweet paprika
2 teaspoons mustard powder
large pinch ground allspice
1²⁄₃ cups puréed tomatoes
1 tablespoon concentrated tomato purée
2 teaspoons finely chopped thyme
2 teaspoons finely chopped oregano
2 bay leaves
2½ tablespoons worcestershire sauce
2 cups scallops without roe
12 oysters
chopped Italian parsley, to serve
cooked long-grain rice, to serve

SHRIMP STOCK
8 cups raw shrimp
1 tablespoon olive oil
1 medium onion, chopped
1 medium carrot, chopped
1 medium celery stalk, chopped
1 medium bay leaf
2 whole cloves
3 medium garlic cloves, bruised
3 parsley stalks
1 medium thyme sprig
½ teaspoon black peppercorns

To make the stock, peel the shrimp, reserving the shells. Gently pull out the dark vein from the back of each shrimp, starting at the head end. Cover the shrimp meat and refrigerate until ready to use. Heat the oil in a large saucepan, add the shrimp shells and cook over high heat for 8 minutes, or until bright orange. Add 2.5 quarts cold water and the remaining stock ingredients and bring to a boil. Reduce the heat to low and simmer for 30 minutes, skimming occasionally, then strain well and set aside — you should have about 8 cups stock.

Meanwhile, heat the olive oil in a frying pan and sauté the okra over medium heat for 10 minutes, or until slightly softened. Remove from the pan and set aside. Add the chorizo to the pan and cook for 5 minutes, or until well browned, then set aside. Add the ham and cook for a few minutes, or until lightly browned.

Heat the extra olive oil in a large saucepan, add the flour and stir to combine. Cook, stirring regularly over medium heat for 30 seconds, or until the roux turns a color somewhere between milk and dark chocolate, but do not allow to burn. Add the onion, celery, pepper and garlic to the roux and cook for about 10 minutes, or until softened. Add the cayenne, paprika, mustard and allspice and stir for 1 minute. Add the puréed tomato, concentrated tomato purée, shrimp stock, thyme, oregano, bay leaves, worcestershire sauce, chorizo and ham and bring to a boil. Reduce the heat to low and simmer for 1 hour then add the okra and continue cooking for a further 1 hour or until the gumbo is thick and glossy.

Add the shrimp, scallops and oysters and cook for about 5–8 minutes, or until all the seafood is cooked through. Stir in the parsley and season to taste. Ladle the soup over the hot rice in individual bowls and serve with lemon wedges, if you like.

Bouillabaisse with Rouille

☙ SERVES 6
☙ PREPARATION TIME: 35 MINUTES
☙ COOKING TIME: 1 HOUR 10 MINUTES

¼ cup olive oil
1 large onion, chopped
2 leeks, white part only, sliced
4 garlic cloves, crushed
1 lb 2 oz ripe tomatoes, peeled, seeded, and roughly chopped
1–2 tablespoons concentrated tomato purée
6 Italian parsley sprigs
2 bay leaves
2 thyme sprigs
1 fennel sprig
2 pinches saffron threads
4 lb 8 oz fish trimmings (such as heads, bones, shellfish remains)
1 tablespoon Pernod or Ricard
4 potatoes, cut into ⅝ inch slices
3 lb 5 oz mixed fish fillets (such as rascasse, snapper, blue eye and bream), cut into large chunks (see Note)
2 tablespoons chopped Italian parsley

TOAST
12 slices of baguette
2 large garlic cloves, sliced in half

ROUILLE
3 slices white bread, crusts removed
1 red pepper, seeded, membrane removed and quartered
1 small red chili, seeded and chopped
3 garlic cloves, crushed
1 tablespoon shredded basil
⅓ cup olive oil

Heat the oil in a large saucepan over medium heat, add the onion and leek and cook for 5 minutes without browning. Add the garlic, tomato, and 1 tablespoon tomato purée, reduce the heat and simmer for 5 minutes. Stir in 8 cups cold water then add the parsley, bay leaves, thyme, fennel, saffron, and fish trimmings. Bring to a boil, then reduce the heat and simmer for 30 minutes. Strain the stock into a large saucepan, pressing the juices out of the ingredients, and reserving 2 tablespoons of stock for the rouille.

Add the Pernod or Ricard to the saucepan and stir in the remaining tomato purée. Season, then bring to a boil and add the potato. Reduce the heat and simmer for 5 minutes. Add the firmer-fleshed fish to the saucepan and cook for 2–3 minutes, then add the more delicate pieces of fish and cook for a further 5 minutes.

Meanwhile, toast the bread until golden on both sides. While warm, rub the surfaces with the garlic.

To make the rouille, soak the bread in cold water for 5 minutes. Cook the pepper pieces, skin side up, under a hot broiler until the skin blackens and blisters. Cool in a plastic bag, then peel. Roughly chop the flesh. Squeeze the bread dry and place in a food processor with the pepper, chili, garlic, and basil. Process to a smooth paste. With the motor running, gradually add the oil until the consistency resembles mayonnaise. Thin with 1–2 tablespoons of the reserved stock. Season to taste.

To serve, place two pieces of toast in each soup bowl. Spoon in the soup and fish. Sprinkle with the parsley. Serve the rouille on the side.

NOTE: Use at least four different fish with a range of textures and flavors. Shellfish such as lobster, crab, scallops or mussels can be used.

Seafood Pie

* SERVES 8
* PREPARATION TIME: 20 MINUTES
* COOKING TIME: 1 HOUR 20 MINUTES

2 tablespoons olive oil
3 large onions, thinly sliced
1 fennel bulb, thinly sliced
2½ cups fish stock
3 cups whipping cream
1 tablespoon brandy
3½ cups skinless snapper fillets,
    cut into large pieces
1 cup scallops
4 cups raw shrimp, peeled and deveined
2 tablespoons chopped Italian parsley
2 sheets frozen puff pastry, thawed
1 egg, lightly beaten

Preheat the oven to 425°F. Heat the oil in a deep frying pan, add the onion and fennel and cook over medium heat for 20 minutes or until caramelized.

Add the stock to the pan and bring to a boil. Cook until the liquid is almost evaporated. Stir in the cream and brandy, bring to a boil, then reduce the heat and simmer for 10 minutes, or until reduced by half. Add the seafood and parsley and toss for 3 minutes.

Lightly grease a 2.5 quart pie dish and add the seafood mixture. Arrange the pastry over the top to cover, trim the excess and press down around the edges. Decorate with any trimmings. Make a steam hole in the top and brush the pastry with egg. Bake for 30 minutes, or until cooked through and the pastry is crisp and golden.

Sri Lankan Fish Fillets in Tomato Curry

❧ SERVES 6
❧ PREPARATION TIME: 20 MINUTES
❧ COOKING TIME: 20 MINUTES

2 lb 4 oz skinless, boneless firm
    white fish fillets
¼ cup vegetable oil
1 large onion, finely chopped
3 large garlic cloves, crushed
2 tablespoons grated fresh ginger
1 teaspoon black mustard seeds
5 cups canned chopped tomatoes
3 tablespoons finely chopped cilantro
2 small green chilies, seeded and finely
    chopped
2 tablespoons grated jaggery or soft
    brown sugar
steamed rice, to serve

MARINADE
¼ cup lemon juice
¼ cup coconut vinegar (see Note)
2 teaspoons cumin seeds
1 teaspoon ground turmeric
1 teaspoon cayenne pepper

To make the marinade, put the lemon juice, coconut vinegar, cumin seeds, ground turmeric, cayenne pepper and 1 teaspoon salt in a shallow, non-metallic container and mix together thoroughly.

Carefully remove any remaining bones from the fish with tweezers and cut the flesh into 1 x 4 inch pieces. Add the fish pieces to the marinade and gently toss until they are well coated. Cover with plastic wrap and refrigerate for 30 minutes.

Heat a non-stick wok over high heat, add the oil and swirl to coat the base and side. Reduce the heat to low, add the onion, garlic, ginger and mustard seeds and cook, stirring frequently, for 5 minutes. Add the fish and marinade, diced tomato, cilantro, chili and jaggery to the wok and cover. Simmer gently, stirring occasionally, for 10–15 minutes, or until the fish is cooked and just flakes when tested with a fork. Serve with steamed rice.

NOTE: Coconut vinegar is made from the sap of various palm trees.

Poached Ocean Trout

* SERVES 8–10
* PREPARATION TIME: 50 MINUTES
* COOKING TIME: 50 MINUTES

8 cups white wine
¼ cup white wine vinegar
2 onions
10 whole cloves
4 carrots, chopped
1 lemon, cut in quarters
2 bay leaves
4 Italian parsley stalks
1 teaspoon whole black peppercorns
5 lb 8 oz ocean trout, cleaned, gutted, and
    scaled
fresh chives, to garnish
1 lemon, thinly sliced, to garnish

DILL MAYONNAISE
1 egg, at room temperature
1 egg yolk, at room temperature
1 tablespoon lemon juice
1 teaspoon white wine vinegar
1½ cups light olive oil
1–2 tablespoons chopped dill

Combine the wine and vinegar in a large heavy-based saucepan with 10 cups water.

Stud the onions with the cloves. Add to the pan with the carrot, lemon, bay leaves, parsley, and peppercorns. Bring to a boil, reduce the heat and simmer for 30–35 minutes. Cool. Strain into a fish kettle that will hold the trout.

Place the whole fish in the fish kettle and add water if necessary, to just cover the fish. Bring to a boil, then reduce the heat to a low simmer, cover and poach gently for 10–15 minutes, until the fish flakes when tested in the thickest part. Remove the kettle from the heat and leave the fish to cool in the liquid.

For the dill mayonnaise, process the egg, yolk, lemon juice, and wine vinegar in a food processor for 10 seconds, or until blended. With the motor running, add the oil in a thin, steady stream, blending until all the oil is added and the mayonnaise is thick and creamy – it should be thick enough to form peaks. Transfer to a bowl and stir in the dill, and salt and pepper, to taste.

Remove the cold fish from the liquid, place on a serving platter and peel back the skin. Garnish with chives and lemon slices. Serve with the dill mayonnaise.

NOTE: Atlantic salmon, snapper, sea bass or red emperor can also be used. If you don't have a fish kettle, use a baking dish big enough to hold the fish, cover with foil and bake in a 350°F oven for 20–30 minutes.

Seafood Risotto

🌿 SERVES 4–6

🌿 PREPARATION TIME: 25 MINUTES

🌿 COOKING TIME: 45 MINUTES

1 lb 2 oz black mussels
1¼ cups dry white wine
5 cups fish stock
pinch saffron threads
2 tablespoons olive oil
1½ tablespoons butter
1 lb 2 oz raw shrimp, peeled and deveined
8 oz squid tubes, sliced into thin rings
7 oz scallops
3 garlic cloves, crushed
1 onion, finely chopped
2 cups risotto rice
2 ripe tomatoes, peeled and roughly
    chopped
2 tablespoons chopped Italian parsley

Scrub the mussels with a stiff brush and pull out the hairy beards. Discard any broken mussels, or open ones that don't close when tapped on the bench. Rinse well. Pour the wine into a large saucepan and bring to a boil over medium heat. Add the mussels, cover, and cook over medium heat for 3–5 minutes, or until the mussels open. Discard any unopened mussels. Strain, reserving the liquid. Remove the mussels from their shells. Combine the mussel liquid, stock, and saffron in a saucepan, cover and keep at a low simmer.

Heat the oil and butter in a saucepan over medium heat. Add the shrimp and cook until pink. Remove. Add the squid and scallops and cook about 1–2 minutes, or until white. Remove. Add the garlic and onion and cook for 3 minutes, or until golden. Add the rice and stir. Add ½ cup of the hot stock, stirring until it is all absorbed. Continue adding stock, ½ cup at a time, stirring, for 25 minutes, or until the liquid is absorbed. Stir in the tomato, seafood, and parsley and heat through. Season to taste.

Balinese Seafood Curry

⚹ SERVES 6
⚹ PREPARATION TIME: 20 MINUTES
⚹ COOKING TIME: 20 MINUTES

3¼ cups raw shrimp
1 tablespoon lime juice
9 oz swordfish, cut into 1¼ inch cubes
9 oz squid tubes, cut into ½ inch rings
¼ cup vegetable oil
2 medium red onions, chopped
2 small red chilies, seeded and sliced
½ cup fish stock
shredded Thai basil, to garnish

CURRY PASTE
2 medium tomatoes
5 small red chilies, seeded and chopped
5 medium garlic cloves, chopped
2 medium lemongrass stems,
    white part only, sliced
1 tablespoon coriander seeds,
    dry-roasted and ground
1 teaspoon shrimp powder,
    dry-roasted (see Notes)
1 tablespoon ground almonds
¼ teaspoon ground nutmeg
1 teaspoon ground turmeric
3 tablespoons tamarind purée

To make the curry paste, score a cross in the base of each tomato. Put in a heatproof bowl and cover with boiling water. Leave for 30 seconds, then transfer to cold water, drain and peel away the skin from the cross. Cut the tomatoes in half, scoop out the seeds and chop the flesh. Put in a food processor with the remaining paste ingredients and blend until a thick paste forms.

Peel the shrimp and gently pull out the dark vein from the back of each shrimp, starting at the head end.

Pour the lime juice into a bowl and season. Add the seafood, coat well and allow to marinate for 20 minutes.

Heat a non-stick wok over high heat, add the oil and swirl to coat the base and side. Add the onion, chili and curry paste, and cook, stirring occasionally, over low heat for 10 minutes, or until fragrant. Add the swordfish and shrimp, and stir to coat in the curry paste mixture. Cook for 3 minutes, or until the shrimp just turn pink, then add the squid and cook for a further 1 minute. Add the stock and bring to a boil, then reduce the heat and simmer for 2 minutes, or until the seafood is cooked and tender. Season to taste and garnish with the shredded fresh basil.

NOTES: If you can't find shrimp powder, put some dried shrimp in a mortar and pestle or small food processor and grind or process into a fine powder. Use a non-stick or stainless-steel wok to cook this recipe as the tamarind will react with the metal in a regular wok and badly taint the dish.

Seared Scallops with Chili Bean Paste

※ SERVES 4
※ PREPARATION TIME: 20 MINUTES
※ COOKING TIME: 15 MINUTES

1 lb 2 oz egg noodles
1/4 cup peanut oil
20 medium scallops, roe removed
1 large onion, cut into thin wedges
3 medium garlic cloves, crushed
1 tablespoon grated fresh ginger
1 tablespoon chili bean paste
5 1/2 oz choy sum, cut into 2 inch lengths
1/4 cup chicken stock
2 tablespoons light soy sauce
2 tablespoons kecap manis (see Note)
1 handful cilantro leaves
1 cup bean sprouts, washed
1 large red chili, seeded and thinly sliced
1 teaspoon sesame oil
1 tablespoon Chinese rice wine

Put the noodles in a heatproof bowl, cover with boiling water and soak for 1 minute to separate. Drain, rinse, then drain again. Set aside.

Heat a wok over high heat, add 2 tablespoons peanut oil and swirl to coat the base and side. Add the scallops in batches and sear for 20 seconds on each side, or until sealed. Remove from the wok and set aside.

Add the remaining peanut oil to the wok and swirl to coat. Stir-fry the onion for 1–2 minutes, or until softened. Add the garlic and ginger and cook for 30 seconds. Stir in the chili bean paste and cook for 1 minute, or until fragrant. Add the choy sum, noodles, stock, soy sauce and kecap manis. Stir-fry for 4 minutes, or until the choy sum has wilted and the noodles have absorbed most of the liquid. Return the scallops to the wok, add the cilantro, bean sprouts, chili, sesame oil and rice wine, tossing gently until combined. Serve immediately.

NOTE: Kecap manis is an Indonesian sweet soy sauce. If you are unable to find it, use soy sauce sweetened with a little unpacked brown sugar.

Indonesian Sambal Squid

☆ SERVES 6
☆ PREPARATION TIME: 20 MINUTES
☆ COOKING TIME: 15 MINUTES

2 lb 4 oz cleaned squid rings
1 tablespoon white vinegar
1 tablespoon tamarind pulp
1/3 cup boiling water
4 medium red Asian shallots, finely
    chopped
8 small red chilies, half of them seeded,
    chopped
6 medium garlic cloves
1 medium lemongrass stem, white part
    only, chopped
2 teaspoons grated fresh ginger
1/2 teaspoon shrimp paste
2 1/2 tablespoons peanut oil
1/2 teaspoon ground cumin
1 1/2 tablespoons unpacked brown sugar
steamed rice, to serve

Cut each squid ring in half lengthways and open out flat, with the inside uppermost. Score a shallow diamond pattern all over the squid rings, taking care not to cut all the way through. Cut the rings into 2 inch squares. Put the pieces in a bowl with the vinegar and 4 cups water and soak for 10 minutes, then rinse and drain the squid and set aside.

Put the tamarind in a bowl and pour in the boiling water. Allow to steep for 5 minutes, breaking up the pulp as it softens. Strain into a bowl and discard the solids.

Put the shallots, chili, garlic, lemongrass, ginger, shrimp paste and 1 teaspoon of the oil in a small food processor or mortar and pestle and blend or pound until a smooth paste is formed. Stir in the cumin.

Heat a non-stick wok over high heat, add 1 tablespoon of the oil and swirl to coat the base and side. Add the paste and cook for 5 minutes, or until it is fragrant, glossy and the liquid has evaporated. Remove from the wok.

Reheat the wok to very hot, add the remaining oil and swirl to coat. Add the squid pieces in small batches and stir-fry for 1–2 minutes, or until cooked through. Remove from the wok.

Reduce the heat to medium, then add the paste, strained tamarind water and sugar. Stir-fry for 2 minutes, or until the sauce ingredients are well combined. Return the squid to the wok and stir-fry for 1 minute, or until the squid is well coated with the sauce and heated through. Serve with steamed rice.

NOTE: Use a non-stick or stainless steel wok to cook this recipe because the tamarind will react with the metal in a regular wok and taint the dish.

Cioppino

❄ SERVES 4
❄ PREPARATION TIME: 30 MINUTES
❄ COOKING TIME: 50 MINUTES

2 dried Chinese mushrooms
2 lb 4 oz skinless firm white fish fillets
    (such as hake, snapper, ocean perch or
    red mullet)
13 oz raw large shrimp
1 raw lobster tail (about 14 oz)
12–15 black mussels
¼ cup olive oil
1 large onion, finely chopped
1 green pepper, seeded and membrane
    removed, finely chopped
2–3 garlic cloves, crushed
1¾ cups canned crushed tomatoes
1 cup dry white wine
1 cup tomato juice
1 cup fish stock
1 bay leaf
2 Italian parsley sprigs
2 teaspoons shredded basil
1 tablespoon chopped Italian parsley,
    to garnish

Place the mushrooms in a small bowl, cover with boiling water, and soak for 20 minutes. Cut the fish into bite-sized pieces, removing any bones.

Peel the shrimp, leaving the tails intact. Gently pull out the dark vein from each shrimp back, starting at the head end.

Starting at the end where the head was, cut down the sides of the lobster shell on the underside of the lobster with kitchen scissors. Pull back the flap, remove the meat from the shell, and cut into small pieces.

Scrub the mussels with a stiff brush and pull out the hairy beards. Discard any broken mussels, or open ones that don't close when tapped on the bench. Rinse well.

Drain the mushrooms, squeeze dry, and chop finely. Heat the oil in a heavy-based saucepan, add the onion, pepper, and garlic and stir over medium heat for about 5 minutes, or until the onion is soft. Add the mushrooms, tomato, wine, tomato juice, stock, bay leaf, parsley sprigs, and basil. Bring to a boil, reduce the heat, then cover and simmer for 30 minutes.

Layer the fish and shrimp in a large frying pan. Add the sauce, then cover and leave on low heat for 10 minutes, or until the shrimp are pink and the fish is cooked. Add the lobster and mussels and simmer for a further 4–5 minutes. Season. Discard any unopened mussels. Sprinkle with the chopped parsley.

Fish Baked in Salt

❀ SERVES 6
❀ PREPARATION TIME: 20 MINUTES
❀ COOKING TIME: 40 MINUTES

4 lb whole fish (such as blue-eye, sea bass, or groper), scaled and cleaned
2 lemons, sliced
4 thyme sprigs, plus extra, to garnish
1 fennel bulb, thinly sliced
6 lb 12 oz rock salt
⅔ cup all-purpose flour

Preheat the oven to 400°F. Rinse the fish and pat dry inside and out with paper towels. Place the lemon, thyme, and fennel inside the cavity.

Pack half the salt into a large baking dish and place the fish on top. Cover with the remaining salt, pressing down until the salt is packed firmly around the fish.

Combine the flour with enough water to form a smooth paste, then brush, spreading carefully and evenly, over the surface of the salt. Be careful not to disturb the salt.

Bake the fish for 30–40 minutes, or until a skewer inserted into the center of the fish comes out hot. Carefully crack open the salt crust with the back of a spoon and gently remove the skin from the fish, ensuring that no salt remains on the flesh. Garnish with thyme.

Stuffed Fish

❀ SERVES 4
❀ PREPARATION TIME: 40 MINUTES
❀ COOKING TIME: 45 MINUTES

2 lb 4 oz whole fish (such as snapper, murray cod, or sea bass), scaled and cleaned
¼ cup lemon juice
1½ tablespoons butter, chopped

STUFFING
2 tablespoons olive oil
1 small onion, finely chopped
3 tablespoons chopped celery leaves
2 tablespoons chopped Italian parsley
1 cup fresh breadcrumbs
1½ tablespoons lemon juice
1 egg, lightly beaten

Preheat the oven to 350°F. Pat the fish dry and sprinkle with salt and the lemon juice. Set aside.

To make the stuffing, heat the oil in a saucepan, add the onion and cook over medium heat for 2 minutes, or until softened. Add the celery leaves and parsley and cook, stirring, for a further 2 minutes. Spoon into a bowl, add the breadcrumbs, lemon juice, and salt, to taste, then mix well. Cool slightly, then stir in the egg.

Place the stuffing in the fish cavity and secure the opening with skewers. Place the fish in a large greased baking dish and dot with butter. Bake for 30–35 minutes, or until the fish is cooked and flakes easily when tested with a fork. The thickness of the fish will determine the cooking time. Transfer to a serving dish.

Fish Baked in Salt

Salmon Stew (Ishikari Nabe)

* SERVES 2–4
* PREPARATION TIME: 20 MINUTES
* COOKING TIME: 40 MINUTES

12 dried shiitake mushrooms
1 1/3 cups firm tofu
1/2 Chinese cabbage
4 salmon cutlets
2 inch pieces canned bamboo
    shoots
8 cups dashi
1/3 cup Japanese soy sauce
1/4 cup mirin or sake

SESAME SEED SAUCE
2/3 cup white sesame seeds
2 teaspoons oil
1/2 cup Japanese soy sauce
2 tablespoons mirin
3 teaspoons sugar
1/2 teaspoon instant dashi granules

Soak the mushrooms in warm water for 15 minutes, then drain. Cut the tofu into 12 squares. Coarsely shred the cabbage into 2 inch wide pieces.

Place the mushrooms, tofu, cabbage, salmon, bamboo shoots, dashi, Japanese soy sauce, mirin and a pinch of salt in a large saucepan and bring to a boil. Reduce the heat, cover and simmer over medium heat for 15 minutes. Turn the salmon cutlets over and simmer for a further 15 minutes, or until tender.

To make the sesame seed sauce, toast the sesame seeds in a frying pan over medium heat for 3–4 minutes, shaking the pan gently, until the seeds are golden brown. Remove from the pan at once to prevent burning. Grind the seeds using a mortar and pestle until a paste is formed. Add the oil, if necessary, to assist in forming a paste. Mix the paste with the Japanese soy sauce, mirin, sugar, dashi granules and 1/2 cup warm water.

Pour the salmon stew into warmed serving bowls and serve with the sesame seed sauce.

NOTE: This dish is traditionally cooked in a clay pot over a burner and served in the same pot. Diners dip the fish and vegetable pieces into the accompanying sauce and the broth is served in small bowls at the end of the meal.

Salmon Steaks with Herb Sauce

❀ SERVES 4
❀ PREPARATION TIME: 25 MINUTES
❀ COOKING TIME: 20 MINUTES

2 tablespoons olive oil
4 x 9 oz salmon steaks

HERB SAUCE
1 ½ cups fish stock
½ cup white wine
3 tablespoons snipped chives
3 tablespoons chopped Italian parsley
2 tablespoons shredded basil
2 tablespoons chopped tarragon
1 cup whipping cream
2 egg yolks

To make the herb sauce, combine the stock and wine in a saucepan and bring to a boil. Boil for 5 minutes or until the liquid has reduced by half. Transfer to a food processor, add the chives, parsley, basil, and tarragon and process for 30 seconds. Return to the pan, then stir in the cream and bring to a boil. Reduce the heat to low and simmer for 5 minutes, or until reduced by half. Place the egg yolks in a food processor and process until smooth. Drizzle in the herb mixture. Process until smooth. Season.

Heat the oil in a frying pan, add the salmon steaks, and cook over medium heat for 3 minutes each side, or until just cooked through. Serve hot with herb sauce.

Tandoori Fish

❧ SERVES 4
❧ PREPARATION TIME: 15 MINUTES
❧ COOKING TIME: 10 MINUTES

4 firm white fish fillets (such as blue-eye,
    snapper or perch)
¼ cup lemon juice
1 onion, finely chopped
2 garlic cloves, crushed
1 tablespoon grated fresh ginger
1 red chili
1 tablespoon garam masala
1 teaspoon paprika
2 cups Greek-style yogurt, plus extra to
    serve
few drops red food coloring (optional)
baby spinach leaves, to serve
lime wedges, to serve

Pat the fish fillets dry with paper towels and arrange in a shallow non-metallic dish. Drizzle the lemon juice over the fish and turn to coat with the juice.

Blend the onion, garlic, ginger, chili, garam masala, paprika, and a pinch of salt, in a blender until smooth. Transfer to a bowl and stir in the yogurt and the food coloring, if using. Spoon the marinade over the fish and turn the fish to coat thoroughly. Cover and refrigerate overnight.

Heat a barbecue plate. Remove the fish from the marinade, shaking off any excess. Cook the cutlets on the barbecue, or under a hot broiler, for 3–4 minutes each side, or until the fish flakes easily when tested with a fork. Serve with extra yogurt, spinach leaves, and lime wedges.

Skewered Swordfish with Lemon Sauce

❧ SERVES 6
❧ PREPARATION TIME: 15 MINUTES
❧ COOKING TIME: 5 MINUTES

MARINADE
⅓ cup lemon juice
2 tablespoons olive oil
1 small red onion, thinly sliced
1 teaspoon paprika
2 bay leaves, crushed
10 sage leaves, torn

3 lb 5 oz swordfish
3 tablespoons chopped Italian parsley
¼ cup olive oil
¼ cup lemon juice

Combine the marinade ingredients with 1 teaspoon salt and some ground black pepper in a bowl. Add the fish, toss to coat with the marinade, then cover and refrigerate for 3 hours, turning the fish occasionally.

Cut the fish into 1¼ inch cubes. Thread onto six metal skewers and cook on a chargrill pan or hot barbecue plate for 5 minutes, turning and brushing with marinade several times.

To make the lemon sauce, combine the parsley, oil, and lemon juice. Serve over the fish.

Tandoori Fish

Salmon Pie

❧ SERVES 4–6
❧ PREPARATION TIME: 25 MINUTES
❧ COOKING TIME: 1 HOUR

¼ cup butter
1 onion, finely chopped
2 cups sliced white mushrooms
2 tablespoons lemon juice
7 oz cooked poached salmon fillet, broken
    into small pieces, or 7¾ oz canned red
    salmon
2 hard-boiled eggs, chopped
2 tablespoons chopped dill
3 tablespoons chopped Italian parsley
1 cup cooked long-grain brown rice
¼ cup whipping cream
13 oz ready-made frozen puff pastry,
    thawed
1 egg, lightly beaten
sour cream, to serve (optional)

Melt half the butter in a frying pan and cook the onion for 5 minutes until soft but not brown. Add the mushroom and cook for 5 minutes. Stir in the lemon juice, then remove from the pan.

Melt the remaining butter in the pan, add the salmon and stir for 2 minutes. Remove from the heat, cool slightly and add the egg, dill, parsley, and salt and pepper, to taste. Mix gently and set aside.

Mix the rice and cream in a small bowl.

Roll out half the pastry to 6 x 10 inches. Trim the pastry neatly, saving the trimmings, and put on a greased baking sheet.

Layer the filling onto the pastry, leaving a 1¼ inch border. Put half the rice into the center of the pastry, then the salmon and egg mixture, followed by the mushroom, then the remaining rice. Brush the pastry border with the egg.

Roll out the other pastry half to 8 x 12 inches and place over the filling. Seal the edges. Make two slits in the top. Decorate with the trimmings and chill for 30 minutes.

Preheat the oven to 400°F. Brush the pie with the egg and bake for 15 minutes. Reduce the oven to 350°F and bake the pie for 25–30 minutes, or until crisp and golden. Serve with sour cream.

NOTE: You will need to cook about ½ cup brown rice for this recipe.

Barbecued Fish with Onions and Ginger

❋ SERVES 4–6
❋ PREPARATION TIME: 25 MINUTES
❋ COOKING TIME: 25 MINUTES

2 lb 4 oz small whole firm white fish,
  cleaned, gutted and scaled
2 teaspoons bottled green peppercorns,
  drained and finely crushed
2 teaspoons chopped red chili
3 teaspoons fish sauce
¼ cup vegetable oil
2 onions, thinly sliced
1½ inch piece fresh ginger, thinly sliced
3 garlic cloves, cut into very thin slivers
2 teaspoons sugar
4 scallions, finely shredded

LEMON AND GARLIC DIPPING SAUCE
¼ cup lemon juice
2 tablespoons fish sauce
1 tablespoon superfine sugar
2 small red chilies, finely chopped
3 garlic cloves, chopped

Wash the fish and pat dry inside and out with paper towels. Cut two or three diagonal slashes into the thickest part on both sides. In a food processor, process the peppercorns, chili, and fish sauce to a paste and brush over the fish. Refrigerate for 20 minutes.

Heat a barbecue hotplate or broiler until very hot and then brush with 1 tablespoon of the oil. Cook the fish for 8 minutes each side, or until the flesh flakes easily. If broiling, don't cook too close to the heat.

While the fish is cooking, heat the remaining oil in a frying pan and stir the onion over medium heat until golden. Add the ginger, garlic, and sugar and cook for 3 minutes. Serve over the fish. Sprinkle with the scallions.

Stir all the dipping sauce ingredients in a bowl until the sugar has dissolved. Serve with the fish.

Fish Cooked in Paper

❋ SERVES 4
❋ PREPARATION TIME: 20 MINUTES
❋ COOKING TIME: 20 MINUTES

4 x 7 oz skinless firm white fish fillets
parchment paper
1 leek, white part only, cut into thin
  batons
4 scallions, shredded
1½ tablespoons butter, softened
1 lemon, cut into 12 very thin slices
2–3 tablespoons lemon juice

Preheat the oven to 350°F. Place each fish fillet in the center of a piece of parchment paper large enough to enclose the fish. Season lightly.

Scatter the leek and scallion over the fish. Top each with a teaspoon of butter and three slices of lemon. Sprinkle with the lemon juice. Bring the paper together and fold over several times. Fold the ends under. Bake on a baking sheet for 20 minutes (the steam will make the paper puff up), or until the fish flakes easily when tested with a fork. Serve as parcels or lift the fish out and pour the juices over the top before serving.

Barbecued Fish with Onions and Ginger

Spanish-Style Rice, Mussel, Shrimp and Chorizo Soup

SERVES 4
PREPARATION TIME: 45 MINUTES
COOKING TIME: 45 MINUTES

1 lb 2 oz raw shrimp
2 lb 4 oz black mussels
1 cup dry sherry
1 tablespoon olive oil
1 red onion, chopped
7 oz chorizo sausage, thinly sliced
4 garlic cloves, crushed
1/2 cup long-grain rice
1 2/3 cups canned chopped tomatoes
8 cups chicken stock
1/2 teaspoon saffron threads
2 bay leaves
1 tablespoon chopped oregano
3 tablespoons chopped Italian parsley

Peel the shrimp, leaving the tails intact. Gently pull out the dark vein from each shrimp back, starting from the head end. Scrub the mussels with a stiff brush and pull out the hairy beards. Discard any broken mussels or open ones that don't close when tapped on the bench. Rinse well.

Put the mussels in a saucepan with the sherry and cook, covered, over high heat for 3 minutes, or until the mussels have opened. Strain the liquid into a bowl and reserve. Discard any unopened mussels. Remove all but eight mussels from their shells and discard the empty shells.

Heat the oil in a large saucepan over medium heat, add the onion and cook for 5 minutes, or until softened but not browned. Add the chorizo and cook for 3–5 minutes, or until browned, then add the garlic and cook for a further 1 minute. Add the rice and stir to coat with the chorizo mixture. Add the reserved cooking liquid and cook for 1 minute before adding the tomatoes, stock, saffron, bay leaves, and oregano. Bring to a boil then reduce the heat and simmer, covered, for 25 minutes.

Add the shrimp and the mussels (except the ones in their shells) to the soup, cover with a lid, and cook for 3 minutes then stir in the parsley. Ladle into four serving bowls, then top each bowl with two mussels still in their shells.

SEAFOOD   73

Tuna Skewers with Moroccan Spices

※ SERVES 4
※ PREPARATION TIME: 20 MINUTES
※ COOKING TIME: 5 MINUTES

1 lb 12 oz tuna steaks
2 tablespoons olive oil
1/2 teaspoon ground cumin
2 teaspoons finely grated lemon zest

CHERMOULA
1/2 teaspoon ground coriander
3 teaspoons ground cumin
2 teaspoons paprika
pinch cayenne pepper
4 garlic cloves, crushed
1/3 cup chopped Italian parsley
1/2 cup chopped cilantro leaves
1/3 cup lemon juice
1/2 cup olive oil
couscous, to serve

If using wooden skewers, soak for about 30 minutes to prevent them from burning during cooking.

Cut the tuna into 1 1/4 inch cubes and put in a shallow non-metallic dish. Combine the oil, cumin, and lemon zest and pour over the tuna. Toss to coat, then cover and marinate in the refrigerator for 10 minutes.

Meanwhile, to make the chermoula, put the ground coriander, cumin, paprika, and cayenne pepper in a small frying pan and cook over medium heat for 30 seconds, or until fragrant. Combine with the remaining chermoula ingredients and set aside.

Thread the tuna onto the skewers. Lightly oil a chargrill pan or hot barbecue plate and cook the skewers for 1 minute on each side for rare, or 2 minutes for medium. Serve the skewers on a bed of couscous with the chermoula drizzled over the tuna.

Trout with Almonds

※ SERVES 2
※ PREPARATION TIME: 25 MINUTES
※ COOKING TIME: 10 MINUTES

2 whole rainbow trout, or baby salmon,
    clean, gutted and scaled
all-purpose flour, for coating
1/4 cup butter
1/4 cup flaked almonds
2 tablespoons lemon juice
1 tablespoon finely chopped Italian parsley
lemon or lime wedges, to serve

Wash the fish and pat dry with paper towels. Open the fish out, skin side up. Run a rolling pin along the backbone, starting at the tail, pressing down gently. Turn the fish over and use scissors to cut through the backbone at each end of the fish. Lift out the backbone. Remove any remaining bones. Trim the fins with scissors. Coat the fish with flour. In a large frying pan, heat half the butter and add the fish. Cook for 4 minutes each side, or until golden brown. Remove the fish and place on heated serving plates. Cover with foil.

Heat the remaining butter, add the almonds, and stir until light golden. Add the lemon juice, parsley, and salt and freshly ground pepper. Stir until the sauce is heated through. Pour over the fish and serve with lemon or lime wedges.

Tuna Skewers with Moroccan Spices

Sweet Chili Shrimp

❀ SERVES 4
❀ PREPARATION TIME: 20 MINUTES
❀ COOKING TIME: 10 MINUTES

1/3 cup chili garlic sauce
2 tablespoons tomato ketchup
2 tablespoons Chinese rice wine
1 tablespoon Chinese black vinegar
1 tablespoon soy sauce
1 tablespoon unpacked brown sugar
1 teaspoon cornstarch
2 lb 4 oz raw shrimp
2 tablespoons peanut oil
1 1/4 inch piece fresh ginger, finely sliced
2 garlic cloves, finely chopped
5 scallions, cut into 1 1/4 inch lengths, plus
    extra, to garnish
steamed rice, to serve

To make the stir-fry sauce, combine the chili garlic sauce, tomato ketchup, rice wine, black vinegar, soy sauce, and sugar in a small bowl. Dissolve the cornstarch in 1/2 cup water and stir into the sauce. Set aside.

Peel the shrimp and gently pull out the dark vein from each shrimp back, starting from the head end.

Heat a wok over high heat, add the oil and swirl to coat the base and side, then add the ginger, garlic, and scallion, and stir fry for 1 minute. Add the shrimp and cook for 2 minutes, or until the shrimp are pink and starting to curl. Remove from the wok.

Pour the stir-fry sauce into the wok and cook, stirring, for 1–2 minutes, or until it thickens slightly. Return the shrimp to the wok for a further 2 minutes, or until heated and cooked through. Garnish with the extra chopped scallion. Serve with steamed rice.

Stir-Fried Fish with Ginger

❀ SERVES 4
❀ PREPARATION TIME: 20 MINUTES
❀ COOKING TIME: 15 MINUTES

1 tablespoon peanut oil
1 small onion, thinly sliced
3 teaspoons ground coriander
1 lb 5 oz boneless white fish fillets, cut
    into bite-sized strips
1 tablespoon finely shredded fresh ginger
1 teaspoon finely chopped and seeded
    green chili
2 tablespoons lime juice
2 tablespoons cilantro leaves
steamed rice, to serve

Heat a wok over high heat, add the oil and swirl to coat the base and side. Add the onion and stir-fry for 4 minutes, or until soft and golden. Add the ground coriander and cook for 1–2 minutes, or until fragrant. Add the fish, ginger, and chili and stir-fry for 5–7 minutes, or until the fish is cooked through, taking care that the fish doesn't break up. Stir in the lime juice and season to taste. Garnish with the cilantro leaves and serve with steamed rice.

Sweet Chili Shrimp

Baked Salmon

❀ SERVES 8
❀ PREPARATION TIME: 10 MINUTES
❀ COOKING TIME: 30 MINUTES

4 lb 8 oz Atlantic salmon, cleaned, gutted
    and scaled
2 scallions, roughly chopped
3 dill sprigs
1/2 lemon, thinly sliced
6 black peppercorns
olive oil, for brushing
1/4 cup dry white wine
3 bay leaves
lemon wedges, to serve

Preheat the oven to 350°F. Wash the salmon under cold running water and pat dry inside and out with paper towels. Stuff the cavity with the scallion, dill, lemon slices, and peppercorns.

Brush a large double-layered piece of foil with oil and lay the salmon on the foil. Sprinkle the wine all over the salmon and arrange the bay leaves over the top. Fold the foil over and wrap up tightly.

Bake in a shallow baking dish for 30 minutes. Turn the oven off and leave the salmon in the oven, with the foil on, for 45 minutes with the door closed.

Undo the foil and carefully peel away the skin of the salmon on the top side. Carefully flip the salmon onto the serving plate and remove the skin from the other side. Pull out the fins and any visible bones. Serve at room temperature with lemon wedges.

Jasmine Tea Steamed Fish

❀ SERVES 4
❀ PREPARATION TIME: 10 MINUTES
❀ COOKING TIME: 25 MINUTES

2 1/3 cups jasmine tea leaves
1 1/2 inch piece fresh ginger, thinly sliced
4 scallions, cut into 2 inch lengths
4 x 7 oz skinless firm white fish fillets

GINGER SCALLION SAUCE
1/2 cup fish stock
1/4 cup light soy sauce
3 scallions, thinly sliced
1 tablespoon finely shredded fresh ginger
2 teaspoons superfine sugar
1 large red chili, sliced

Line a double bamboo steamer with parchment paper. Place the tea, ginger, and scallion in a layer on the bottom steamer basket. Cover and steam over a wok of simmering water for 10 minutes, or until the tea is moist and fragrant.

Lay the fish in a single layer in the top steamer basket and steam for 5–10 minutes, or until the fish flakes easily when tested with a fork.

To make the sauce, combine all the ingredients in a small saucepan with 1/2 cup water. Heat over low heat for 5 minutes, or until the sugar has dissolved. Drizzle the fish with the sauce and serve with steamed rice, if desired.

Baked Salmon

Chorba Bil Hout

❀ SERVES 6
❀ PREPARATION TIME: 30 MINUTES
❀ COOKING TIME: 30 MINUTES

2 red peppers, quartered, seeded, and
   membrane removed
1 long fresh red chili, seeded
2 tablespoons extra virgin olive oil
1 brown onion, finely chopped
1 tablespoon concentrated tomato purée
2–3 teaspoons harissa
4 garlic cloves, finely chopped
2 teaspoons ground cumin
3 cups fish stock
$1^2/_3$ cups canned crushed tomatoes
1 lb 10 oz skinless firm white fish fillets
   (such as blue eye or ling), cut into
   $^3/_4$ inch squares
2 bay leaves
2 tablespoons chopped cilantro leaves
6 thick slices baguette
1 garlic clove, halved

Broil the pepper and chili until the skin is blackened
and blistered. Cool in a plastic bag, then peel and cut
into thin strips.

Heat the oil in a large saucepan and cook the onion
for 5 minutes, or until softened. Add the tomato purée,
harissa, garlic, cumin, and $^1/_2$ cup water, then stir to
combine. Add the fish stock, tomatoes and 2 cups water.
Bring to a boil, then reduce the heat and add the fish
and bay leaves. Simmer for 7–8 minutes, or until the
fish is just cooked. Remove the fish with a slotted spoon
and place on a plate. Discard the bay leaves. When the
soup has cooled slightly, add half the chopped cilantro
and purée in batches, in a food processor, until smooth.
Season to taste.

Return the soup to the pan, add the fish, pepper, and
chili and simmer gently while you prepare the toast.

Toast the bread and, while still warm, rub with the cut
garlic. Place one slice of toast in each soup bowl and
pile several pieces of fish on top. Ladle the soup over
the top, distributing the pepper evenly. Garnish with the
remaining cilantro.

NOTE: Chorba Bil Hout is a traditional Moroccan fish soup, robustly
flavored with garlic, chili, and harissa.

poultry

Roasted Rosemary Chicken

* SERVES 4
* PREPARATION TIME: 15 MINUTES
* COOKING TIME: 1 HOUR

3 lb 5 oz–4 lb whole chicken
6 large rosemary sprigs
4 garlic cloves
¼ cup olive oil

Preheat the oven to 425°F. Wipe the chicken inside and out and pat dry with paper towels. Season the chicken cavity and place four rosemary sprigs and the garlic cloves inside.

Rub the outside of the chicken with 1 tablespoon of the oil, season, and place the chicken on its side in a roasting pan. Put the remaining rosemary sprigs in the pan and drizzle the remaining oil around the pan.

Place the pan on the middle shelf in the oven. After 20 minutes, turn the chicken onto the other side, baste with the juices and cook for a further 20 minutes. Turn the chicken, breast side up, baste again and cook for a further 15 minutes, or until the juices between the body and thigh run clear when pierced with a knife. Transfer the chicken to a warm serving dish and set aside for at least 10 minutes before carving.

Meanwhile, pour off most of the fat from the roasting pan and return the pan to the stovetop over high heat. Add 2 tablespoons water and, using a wooden spoon, scrape the base of the pan to loosen the residue. Check the seasoning and pour over the chicken to serve.

Canja

10 cups chicken stock
1 onion, cut into thin wedges
1 celery stalk, finely chopped
1 teaspoon grated lemon zest
3 tomatoes, peeled, seeded, and roughly
    chopped
1 mint sprig
1 tablespoon olive oil
2 boneless, skinless chicken breasts
1 cup long-grain rice
2 tablespoons lemon juice
2 tablespoons chopped mint

Combine the stock, onion, celery, lemon zest, tomato, mint, and olive oil in a large saucepan. Slowly bring to a boil then reduce the heat, add the chicken and simmer gently for 20–25 minutes, or until the chicken is cooked through.

Remove the chicken from the saucepan and discard the mint sprig. Allow the chicken to cool, then thinly slice.

Meanwhile, add the rice to the pan and simmer for 25–30 minutes, or until the rice is tender. Return the sliced chicken to the pan, add the lemon juice, and stir for 1–2 minutes, or until the chicken is warmed through. Season to taste and stir in the chopped mint just before serving.

NOTE: Canja is a hearty Brazilian soup made with chicken and rice, and flavored with garlic and lemon.

Herbed Poussins

4¾ oz butter, softened
2 teaspoons chopped lemon thyme
1 tablespoon chopped Italian parsley
2 scallions, finely chopped
1 teaspoon finely grated lemon zest
1½ tablespoons lemon juice, plus
    2 teaspoons extra
4 x 1 lb 2 oz baby chickens (poussins)
1½ tablespoons butter, melted

Mix the softened butter with the herbs, scallion, lemon zest, lemon juice, and plenty of salt and pepper.

Preheat the oven to 400°F. Cut the chickens down either side of the backbone. Discard the backbone, and gently flatten the chickens. Carefully lift the skin from the breastbone and the legs and push the herb butter underneath. Tuck in the wings and neck.

Place the chickens on a rack in a baking dish. Brush with the combined melted butter and extra lemon juice. Bake for 30–35 minutes, or until the juices run clear.

Canja

Hainanese Chicken Rice

❀ SERVES 6
❀ PREPARATION TIME: 50 MINUTES
❀ COOKING TIME: 1 HOUR 30 MINUTES

4 lb 8 oz chicken
6 medium scallions
thick slices ginger
4 medium garlic cloves, bruised
1 teaspoon vegetable oil
1 teaspoon sesame oil

RICE
5 medium red Asian shallots, finely
   chopped
2 medium garlic cloves, crushed
1 tablespoon very finely chopped
   fresh ginger
1½ cups jasmine rice
½ cup long-grain glutinous rice
3 plum tomatoes, cut into thin wedges
3 small cucumbers, sliced diagonally
cilantro sprigs, to garnish

SAUCE
2 small red chilies, seeded and chopped
4 medium garlic cloves, roughly chopped
1½ tablespoons finely chopped
   fresh ginger
3 cilantro stems, chopped
2 tablespoons dark soy sauce
2 tablespoons lime juice
2 tablespoons sugar
pinch ground white pepper

Remove the excess fat from around the cavity of the chicken and reserve. Rinse and salt the inside of the chicken and rinse again. Insert the scallions, ginger slices and garlic into the chicken cavity then place, breast side down, in a large saucepan and cover with cold water. Add 1 teaspoon salt and bring to a boil over high heat, skimming the surface as required. Reduce the heat to low and simmer gently for 15 minutes, then carefully turn over without piercing the skin and cook for another 15 minutes, or until the thigh juices run clear when pierced.

Carefully lift the chicken out of the saucepan, draining any liquid from the cavity into the rest of the stock. Reserve 4 cups of the stock. Plunge the chicken into iced water for 5 minutes to stop the cooking process and to firm the skin. Rub the entire surface of the chicken with the combined vegetable and sesame oils and allow to cool while you make the rice.

To make the rice, cook the reserved chicken fat in a saucepan over medium heat for about 8 minutes, or until you have about 2 tablespoons of liquid fat, then discard the solids. (If you prefer, use vegetable oil.) Add the shallots and cook for a few minutes, or until lightly golden, then add the garlic and ginger and stir until fragrant. Add both rices and cook for 5 minutes, or until lightly golden, then pour in the reserved chicken stock and 1 teaspoon salt and bring to a boil. Cover and reduce the heat to low and cook for about 20 minutes, or until tender and the liquid has evaporated. Cool, covered, for 10 minutes, then fluff with a fork.

Meanwhile, to make the sauce, pound the chili, garlic, ginger and cilantro stem into a paste using a mortar and pestle. Stir in the rest of the ingredients and season to taste.

Shred the chicken. Divide the rice into six slightly wetted Chinese soup bowls and press down firmly, then turn out onto serving plates. Serve the chicken on a platter with the tomato, cucumber and cilantro and pour the dipping sauce into a small bowl and let your guests help themselves.

General Tso's Chicken

☆ SERVES 4–6
☆ PREPARATION TIME: 15 MINUTES
☆ COOKING TIME: 10 MINUTES

2 tablespoons Chinese rice wine
1 tablespoon cornstarch
1/3 cup dark soy sauce
3 teaspoons sesame oil
3 3/4 cups cubed boneless, skinless chicken
    thighs
2 pieces dried citrus peel
1/2 cup peanut oil
1 1/2–2 teaspoons chili flakes
2 tablespoons finely chopped fresh ginger
1 cup thinly sliced scallions, plus extra,
    to garnish
2 teaspoons sugar
steamed rice, to serve

Combine the rice wine, cornstarch, 2 tablespoons of the soy sauce and 2 teaspoons of the sesame oil in a large non-metallic bowl. Add the chicken, toss to coat in the marinade, then cover and marinate in the refrigerator for 1 hour.

Meanwhile, soak the dried citrus peel in warm water for 20 minutes. Remove from the water and finely chop — you will need 1 1/2 teaspoons chopped peel.

Heat the peanut oil in a wok over high heat. Using a slotted spoon, drain the chicken from the marinade, then add to the wok in batches and stir-fry for 2 minutes at a time, or until browned and just cooked through. Remove from the oil with a slotted spoon and leave to drain in a colander or sieve.

Drain all the oil except 1 tablespoon from the wok. Reheat the wok over high heat, then add the chili flakes and ginger. Stir-fry for 10 seconds, then return the chicken to the wok. Add the scallions, sugar, chopped citrus peel, remaining soy sauce and sesame oil and 1/2 teaspoon salt and stir-fry for a further 2–3 minutes, or until well combined and warmed through. Garnish with the extra scallions and serve with steamed rice.

NOTE: This dish is named after a 19th-century Chinese general from Yunnan province.

Chicken with Forty Cloves of Garlic

❀ SERVES 4
❀ PREPARATION TIME: 20 MINUTES
❀ COOKING TIME: 1 HOUR 40 MINUTES

2/3 tablespoon butter
1 tablespoon olive oil
1 large chicken
40 medium garlic cloves, unpeeled
2 tablespoons chopped rosemary
2 medium thyme sprigs
9 1/2 fl oz dry white wine
2/3 cup chicken stock
1 3/4 cups all-purpose flour

Preheat the oven to 350°F. Melt the butter and oil in a 4.5 quart flameproof casserole dish, then brown the chicken over medium heat until golden all over. Remove the chicken and add the garlic, rosemary and thyme and cook together for 1 minute. Return the chicken to the dish and add the wine and chicken stock. Bring to a simmer, basting the chicken with the sauce.

Put the flour in a bowl and add up to 2/3 cup water to form a pliable paste. Divide into four and roll into cylinder shapes. Place around the rim of the casserole. Put the lid on the dish, pressing down to form a seal. Bake for 1 1/4 hours. Remove the lid by cracking the paste. Return the chicken to the oven to brown for 15 minutes, then transfer to a plate. Reduce the juices to 1 cup over medium heat. Carve the chicken, pierce the garlic skins and squeeze the flesh onto the chicken. Serve with the sauce.

Chicken with Peppers and Olives

❀ SERVES 4
❀ PREPARATION TIME: 30 MINUTES
❀ COOKING TIME: 1 HOUR 10 MINUTES

6 medium tomatoes
3 lb 5 oz chicken, cut into 8 portions
1/4 cup olive oil
2 large red onions, sliced into 1/4 inch slices
2 medium garlic cloves, crushed
3 medium red bell peppers, seeded and membrane removed, cut into 1/2 inch strips
1/3 cup thickly sliced prosciutto, finely chopped
1 tablespoon chopped thyme
2 teaspoons sweet paprika
8 pitted medium black olives
8 pitted medium green olives

Score a cross in the base of each tomato. Put in a heatproof bowl and cover with boiling water. Leave for 30 seconds, then transfer to cold water and peel the skin away from the cross. Cut each tomato in half, scoop out the seeds and finely chop the flesh.

Pat the chicken dry with paper towels and season. Heat the oil in a heavy-based frying pan and cook the chicken a few pieces at a time, skin side down, for 4–5 minutes, until golden. Turn the chicken over and cook for another 2–3 minutes. Transfer to a plate.

Add the onion, garlic, peppers, prosciutto and thyme to the pan. Cook over medium heat, stirring frequently for 8–10 minutes. Add the tomato and paprika, increase the heat and cook for 10–12 minutes, until sauce is thick. Return the chicken to the pan and coat with the sauce. Cover the pan, reduce the heat and simmer the chicken for 25–30 minutes. Add the olives.

Chicken with Forty Cloves of Garlic

Roast Turkey with Rice and Chestnut Stuffing

※ SERVES 6–8
※ PREPARATION TIME: 30 MINUTES
※ COOKING TIME: 3 HOURS 30 MINUTES

6 lb 12 oz turkey, neck and giblets
    removed
1 large red onion, cut into 4–5 slices
2 tablespoons softened butter
1 1/2 cups dry white wine
1 medium carrot, quartered
1 medium celery stalk, quartered
1 large rosemary sprig
2 teaspoons finely chopped thyme
1 cup chicken stock
2 tablespoons all-purpose flour

STUFFING
12 prunes, pitted
1 cups whole fresh chestnuts
2 2/3 tablespoons butter
1 medium red onion, finely chopped
2 medium garlic cloves, crushed
1/3 cup finely chopped pancetta
    (including any fat)
1/2 cup wild rice blend
1/4 cup chicken stock
3 dried juniper berries, lightly crushed
2 teaspoons finely chopped rosemary
3 teaspoons finely chopped thyme

Preheat the oven to 325°F. Soak the prunes in hot water for 20 minutes. Meanwhile, to prepare the chestnuts, make a small cut in the skin on the flat side, put under a hot broiler and cook on both sides until well browned. Put the hot chestnuts in a bowl lined with a damp dish towel and cover with the towel. Leave until cool enough to handle, then peel. Do not allow the chestnuts to cool completely before peeling. Roughly chop the prunes and chestnuts and set aside.

To make the stuffing, melt the butter in a large saucepan and add the onion, garlic and pancetta. Cook over low heat for 5–6 minutes, or until the onion is softened but not brown. Add the rice, stock, juniper berries, prunes and chestnuts, stir well, then pour in 1 1/2 cups water. Bring to a boil and cook, covered, stirring once or twice, for 20–25 minutes, or until the rice is tender and all liquid has been absorbed. Remove from the heat, stir in the rosemary and thyme, and season.

Wash and pat the turkey dry. Fill the cavity with the stuffing. Cross the turkey legs and tie them together, then tuck the wings underneath the body. Arrange the onion slices in the center of a large roasting pan, then sit the turkey on top, breast side up. Season and dot with butter. Pour 1 cup of the wine into the pan, then scatter the carrot, celery, rosemary and 1 teaspoon of thyme.

Roast for 2–2 1/2 hours, or until cooked through and the juices run clear, basting every 30 minutes. After 1 hour, pour half the chicken stock into the pan. Once the skin becomes golden brown, cover with buttered foil.

When cooked, transfer the turkey to a carving plate, cover with foil and leave to rest in a warm spot. Meanwhile, pour the juices into a small saucepan and reduce for 8–10 minutes. Stir in the flour, then add the stock, a little at a time, stirring to form a paste. Slowly add the rest of the stock and wine, stirring so that no lumps form. Stir in the remaining thyme. Bring to a boil and continue to simmer for 6–8 minutes, or until reduced by one-third. Season. Transfer to a gravy boat. Carve the turkey and serve with the stuffing and gravy.

Chicken Chow Mein

⚘ SERVES 4
⚘ PREPARATION TIME: 15 MINUTES
⚘ COOKING TIME: 40 MINUTES

9 oz fresh thin egg noodles
2 teaspoons sesame oil
1/2 cup peanut oil
1 tablespoon Chinese rice wine
1 1/2 tablespoons light soy sauce
3 teaspoons cornstarch
14 oz boneless, skinless chicken breasts,
    cut into thin strips
1 garlic clove, crushed
1 tablespoon finely chopped fresh ginger
3 1/2 oz sugar snap peas, trimmed
3 1/2 cups shredded Chinese cabbage
    (wong bok)
4 scallions, cut into 3/4 inch lengths
3 1/2 fl oz chicken stock
1 1/2 tablespoons oyster sauce
1 cup bean sprouts
1 small red chili, seeded and very thinly
    sliced, to garnish (optional)

Cook the noodles in a saucepan of boiling water for 1 minute, or until tender. Drain well. Add the sesame oil and 1 tablespoon of the peanut oil and toss well. Place on a baking sheet and spread out in a thin layer. Leave in a dry place for at least 1 hour.

Meanwhile, combine the rice wine, 1 tablespoon soy sauce and 1 teaspoon cornstarch in a large non-metallic bowl. Add the chicken and toss well to coat in the marinade. Cover with plastic wrap and marinate for 10 minutes.

Heat 1 tablespoon of the peanut oil in a small non-stick frying pan over high heat. Add one-quarter of the noodles, shaping them into a pancake. Reduce the heat to medium and cook for 4 minutes on each side, or until crisp and golden. Drain on crumpled paper towels and keep warm. Repeat with 3 tablespoons of the oil and the remaining noodles to make four noodle cakes in total.

Heat a wok over high heat, add the remaining peanut oil and swirl to coat the base and side. Stir-fry the garlic and ginger for 30 seconds, then add the chicken and stir-fry for 3–4 minutes, or until golden and tender. Add the sugar snap peas, Chinese cabbage and scallion and stir-fry for 2 minutes, or until the cabbage has wilted. Stir in the stock, oyster sauce, and bean sprouts and bring to a boil.

Combine the remaining cornstarch with 1–2 teaspoons cold water. Stir the cornstarch mixture into the wok along with the remaining soy sauce and cook for 1–2 minutes, or until the sauce thickens.

To assemble, place a noodle cake on each serving plate and then spoon the chicken and vegetable mixture on top. Serve immediately, garnished with chili, if desired.

Chicken Pie with Feta

❀ SERVES 6
❀ PREPARATION TIME: 30 MINUTES
❀ COOKING TIME: 1 HOUR 10 MINUTES

2 lb 4 oz boneless, skinless chicken
    breast
2 cups chicken stock
1/4 cup butter
2 medium scallions, finely chopped
1/2 cup all-purpose flour
1/2 cup whole milk
8 sheets filo pastry (12 x 16 inches)
1/4 cup melted butter, extra
1 1/3 cups crumbled feta
1 tablespoon chopped dill
1 tablespoon snipped chives
1/4 teaspoon freshly grated nutmeg
1 egg, lightly beaten

Cut the chicken into bite-sized pieces. Pour the stock into a saucepan and bring to a boil over high heat. Reduce the heat to low, add the chicken and poach gently for 10–15 minutes, or until the chicken is cooked through. Drain, reserving the stock. Add enough water to the stock in order to bring the quantity up to 2 cups. Preheat the oven to 350°F.

Melt the butter in a saucepan over low heat, add the scallions and cook, stirring, for 5 minutes. Add the flour and stir for 30 seconds. Remove the pan from the heat and gradually add the chicken stock and milk, stirring after each addition. Return to the heat and gently bring to a boil, stirring. Simmer for a few minutes, or until the sauce thickens. Remove from the heat.

Line an ovenproof dish measuring 1 1/2 x 7 x 10 inches with four sheets of filo pastry, brushing one side of each sheet with melted butter as you go. Place the buttered side down. The filo will overlap the edges of the dish. Cover the unused filo with a damp dish towel to prevent it drying out.

Stir the chicken, feta, dill, chives, nutmeg and egg into the sauce. Season to taste. Stack the mixture on top of the filo pastry in the dish. Fold the overlapping filo over the filling and cover the top of the pie with the remaining four sheets of filo, brushing each sheet with melted butter as you go. Scrunch the edges of the filo so they fit in the dish. Brush the top with butter. Bake for 45–50 minutes, or until the pastry is golden brown and crisp.

NOTE: If you prefer, you can use puff pastry instead of filo pastry. If you do so, bake in a 425°F oven for 15 minutes, then reduce the temperature to 350°F and cook for another 30 minutes, or until the pastry is golden.

Roast Duck with Olives

❀ SERVES 4
❀ PREPARATION TIME: 30 MINUTES
❀ COOKING TIME: 1 HOUR 30 MINUTES

SAUCE

1 tablespoon olive oil
1 onion, chopped
1 garlic clove, crushed
2 ripe plum tomatoes, peeled, seeded, and
    finely chopped
1 cup Riesling
2 teaspoons thyme
1 bay leaf
24 niçoise olives, pitted

STUFFING

1/3 cup medium-grain white rice, cooked
1 garlic clove, crushed
3 1/2 oz frozen chopped spinach, defrosted
2 x 3 1/2 oz ducks' livers, chopped
1 egg, lightly beaten
1 teaspoon thyme

4 lb duck
2 bay leaves

Preheat the oven to 400°F. To make the sauce, heat the oil in a frying pan, add the onion and cook for 5 minutes, or until transparent. Add the garlic, tomato, wine, herbs, and season with salt and pepper. Cook for 5 minutes, then add the olives before removing from the heat.

To make the stuffing, thoroughly mix all the ingredients in a bowl and season well. Before stuffing the duck, rinse out the cavity with cold water and pat dry inside and out with paper towels. Put the bay leaves in the cavity, then spoon in the stuffing.

Tuck the wings under the duck, then close the flaps of fat over the parson's nose and secure with a skewer or toothpick. Place in a deep roasting pan and rub 1 teaspoon salt into the skin. Prick the skin all over with a skewer.

Roast on the top shelf of the oven for 35–40 minutes, then carefully pour off the excess fat. Roast for another 35–40 minutes. To check that the duck is cooked, gently pull away one leg from the side. The flesh should be pale brown with no blood in the juices. Carve the duck, then serve with a spoonful of the stuffing, and top with the sauce.

Chicken Laksa

* SERVES 4–6
* PREPARATION TIME: 30 MINUTES
* COOKING TIME: 35 MINUTES

1 1/2 tablespoons coriander seeds
1 tablespoon cumin seeds
1 teaspoon ground turmeric
1 medium onion, roughly chopped
1 tablespoon roughly chopped fresh ginger
3 medium garlic cloves
3 medium lemongrass stems, white part
   only, sliced
6 macadamia nuts
4–6 small red chilies
3 teaspoons shrimp paste, roasted
   (see Note)
4 cups chicken stock
1/4 cup oil
1 3/4 cups chicken thigh fillets, cut into
   3/4 inch pieces
3 cups coconut milk
4 kaffir lime leaves
2 1/2 tablespoons lime juice
2 tablespoons fish sauce
2 tablespoons grated jaggery
   or unpacked brown sugar
2 1/2 cups dried rice vermicelli
1 cup trimmed bean sprouts
4 fried tofu puffs, cut into thin batons
3 tablespoons chopped Vietnamese mint
1 handful cilantro leaves
lime wedges, to serve

Toast the coriander and cumin seeds in a frying pan over medium heat for 1–2 minutes, or until fragrant, tossing the pan constantly to prevent the seeds from burning. Grind finely using a mortar and pestle or a spice grinder.

Put all the spices, onion, ginger, garlic, lemongrass, macadamia nuts, chilies and shrimp paste in a food processor or blender. Add 1/2 cup of the stock and blend to a paste.

Heat the oil in a wok or large saucepan over low heat and gently cook the paste for 3–5 minutes, stirring constantly to prevent it burning or sticking to the bottom of the pan. Add the remaining stock and bring to a boil over high heat. Reduce the heat to medium and simmer for 15 minutes, or until reduced slightly. Add the chicken and simmer for 4–5 minutes. Add the coconut milk, lime leaves, lime juice, fish sauce and jaggery and simmer for 5 minutes over medium–low heat. Do not bring to a boil or cover with a lid, as the coconut milk will split.

Meanwhile, put the vermicelli in a heatproof bowl, cover with boiling water and soak for 6–7 minutes, or until softened. Drain and divide among large serving bowls with the bean sprouts. Ladle the hot soup over the top and garnish with some tofu strips, mint and cilantro leaves. Serve with a wedge of lime.

NOTE: To roast the shrimp paste, wrap the paste in foil and put under a hot broiler for 1 minute.

Chicken Caccitore

❧ SERVES 4
❧ PREPARATION TIME: 15 MINUTES
❧ COOKING TIME: 1 HOUR

¼ cup olive oil

1 large onion, finely chopped

3 medium garlic cloves, crushed

5½ oz finely chopped pancetta

1⅓ cups thickly sliced white mushrooms

1 large chicken (at least 3 lb 8 oz),
    cut into 8 pieces

⅓ cup dry vermouth or dry white wine

3¼ cups canned chopped tomatoes

¼ teaspoon unpacked brown sugar

¼ teaspoon cayenne pepper

1 medium oregano sprig

1 medium thyme sprig

1 medium bay leaf

Heat half the olive oil in a large flameproof casserole dish. Add the onion and garlic and cook for 6–8 minutes over low heat, stirring, until the onion is golden. Add the pancetta and mushrooms, increase the heat and cook, stirring, for 4–5 minutes. Transfer to a bowl.

Add the remaining oil to the casserole dish and brown the chicken pieces, a few at a time, over medium heat. Season as they brown. Spoon off the excess fat and return all the chicken to the casserole dish. Increase the heat, add the vermouth to the dish and cook until the liquid has almost evaporated.

Add the chopped tomato, brown sugar, cayenne pepper, oregano, thyme and bay leaf, and stir in ⅓ cup water. Bring to a boil, then stir in the reserved onion mixture. Reduce the heat, cover and simmer for 25 minutes, or until the chicken is tender but not falling off the bone.

If the liquid is too thin, remove the chicken from the casserole dish, increase the heat and boil until the liquid has thickened. Discard the sprigs of herbs and adjust the seasoning.

Chicken, Thai Basil and Cashew Stir~Fry

※ SERVES 4

※ PREPARATION TIME: 15 MINUTES

※ COOKING TIME: 10 MINUTES

4 cups boneless, skinless chicken breast,
    cut into strips
2 medium lemongrass stems, white part
    only, finely chopped
3 small red chilies, seeded and chopped
4 medium garlic cloves, crushed
1 tablespoon finely chopped fresh ginger
2 cilantro stems, finely chopped
2 tablespoons oil
²/₃ cup cashew nuts
1 ½ tablespoons lime juice
2 tablespoons fish sauce
1 ½ tablespoons grated jaggery or
    unpacked brown sugar
2 very large handfuls Thai basil
2 teaspoons cornstarch

Put the chicken in a large bowl with the lemongrass, chili, garlic, ginger and cilantro stem. Mix together well.

Heat a wok over medium heat, add 1 teaspoon of the oil and swirl to coat. Add the cashews and cook for 1 minute, or until lightly golden. Remove and drain on crumpled paper towels.

Heat the remaining oil in the wok, add the chicken in batches and stir-fry over medium heat for 4–5 minutes, or until browned. Return the chicken to the wok.

Stir in the lime juice, fish sauce, jaggery and basil, and cook for 30–60 seconds, or until the basil just begins to wilt. Mix the cornstarch with 1 tablespoon water, add to the wok and stir until the mixture thickens slightly. Stir in the cashews and serve with steamed rice.

Chicken Braised with Ginger and Star Anise

※ SERVES 4

※ PREPARATION TIME: 10 MINUTES

※ COOKING TIME: 30 MINUTES

1 teaspoon sichuan peppercorns
2 tablespoons peanut oil
³/₄ x 1 ¼ inch piece ginger, cut into thin
    batons
2 medium garlic cloves, chopped
2 lb 4 oz boneless, skinless chicken
    thighs, halved
¹/₃ cup Chinese rice wine
1 tablespoon honey
¹/₄ cup light soy sauce
1 star anise

Heat a wok over medium heat, add the peppercorns and cook, stirring often, for 2–4 minutes, or until fragrant. Remove and lightly crush with the back of a knife.

Reheat the wok, add the oil and swirl to coat. Add the ginger and garlic and cook over low heat for 1–2 minutes, or until lightly golden. Add the chicken, increase the heat to medium and cook for 3 minutes, or until browned all over.

Add the remaining ingredients, reduce the heat and simmer, covered, for 20 minutes, or until the chicken is tender. Serve with rice.

Chicken, Thai Basil and Cashew Stir-Fry

Turkey Roll with Mandarin Sauce

❧ SERVES 8
❧ PREPARATION TIME: 1 HOUR
❧ COOKING TIME: 2 HOURS

$1/2$ cup dried apricots, chopped
$1 1/2$ tablespoons butter
1 onion, finely chopped
1 garlic clove, crushed
14 oz ground chicken
$1 1/2$ cups fresh breadcrumbs
$1/2$ cup currants
$1/4$ cup pistachio nuts, toasted and chopped
3 tablespoons chopped Italian parsley
7 lb 13 oz turkey, boned
olive oil, for rubbing

MANDARIN SAUCE
2 mandarins
1 tablespoon long strips of mandarin zest
2 tablespoons sugar
1 tablespoon brandy
1 cup mandarin juice
$1/3$ cup chicken stock
3 teaspoons cornstarch
1 scallion, finely sliced

Place the apricots in a small bowl, cover with boiling water and soak for 30 minutes. Preheat the oven to 350°F.

Meanwhile, melt the butter in a frying pan, add the onion and garlic and cook, stirring, for about 5 minutes, or until the onion is soft. Remove from the heat. Combine the chicken, onion mixture, breadcrumbs, currants, nuts, parsley, and apricots in a bowl and mix well. Season. Place the turkey on the work surface, skin side down, and form the stuffing mixture into a large sausage shape about the same length as the turkey. Fold the turkey over to enclose the stuffing. Secure with toothpicks or skewers and truss with kitchen string at $1 1/4$ inch intervals.

Place on a lightly greased baking sheet. Rub with a little oil and season. Roast the turkey roll for $1 1/2$–2 hours, or until the juices run clear. Cover and set aside for 10 minutes while preparing the sauce.

To make the mandarin sauce, segment the mandarins. Remove the zest and white pith, then cut between the membranes to release the segments. Place the zest in a saucepan, cover with water, and bring to a boil. Drain and repeat. Sprinkle the sugar over the base of a saucepan over medium heat and stir until all the sugar has dissolved. Remove from the heat, cool, then stir in the brandy. Return to the heat, stir to dissolve any toffee, then add the combined mandarin juice and chicken stock. Add the combined cornstarch and 1 tablespoon water and stir over heat until the mixture thickens. Add the mandarin segments and zest, stirring until heated through. Stir in the scallion, then season.

Carefully remove the string and toothpicks from the Turkey. Cut into slices and serve with the mandarin sauce spooned on top.

Mild Vietnamese Chicken Curry

🌿 SERVES 6
🌿 PREPARATION TIME: 30 MINUTES
🌿 COOKING TIME: 1 HOUR 10 MINUTES

4 1/2 oz dried rice vermicelli
3/4 cup vegetable oil
4 large chicken quarters (leg and thigh),
   skin and excess fat removed, cut into
   thirds
1 tablespoon curry powder
1 teaspoon superfine sugar
1/3 cup vegetable oil, extra
1 lb 2 oz sweet potato, peeled, cut into
   1 1/4 inch cubes
1 large onion, cut into thin wedges
4 garlic cloves, chopped
1 lemon grass stem, white part only, finely
   chopped
2 bay leaves
1 large carrot, cut into 1/2 inch pieces
1 2/3 cups coconut milk

Break the vermicelli into short lengths. Heat half the oil in a wok over medium heat. Cook the vermicelli in batches until crisp, adding more oil when necessary. Drain on paper towels and set aside.

Pat the chicken dry with paper towels. Put the curry powder, sugar, 1/2 teaspoon black pepper, and 2 teaspoons salt in a bowl, and mix together well. Rub the curry mixture onto the chicken pieces then place the chicken on a plate, cover with plastic wrap and refrigerate overnight.

Heat a wok over high heat, add the oil and swirl to coat the base and side. Add the sweet potato and cook over medium heat for 3 minutes, or until lightly golden. Remove with a slotted spoon and set aside.

Remove all but 2 tablespoons of the oil from the wok. Add the onion and cook, stirring, for 5 minutes. Add the garlic, lemon grass, and bay leaves, and cook for 2 minutes. Add the chicken and cook, stirring, over medium heat for 5 minutes, or until well coated in the mixture and starting to change color.

Add 1 cup water and simmer, covered, over low heat for 20 minutes, stirring occasionally. Add the carrot, sweet potato, and coconut milk, and simmer, uncovered, stirring occasionally, for 30 minutes, or until the chicken is cooked and tender. Be careful not to break up the sweet potato cubes. Serve with the crisp vermicelli.

Cantonese Lemon Chicken

* SERVES 4
* PREPARATION TIME: 15 MINUTES
* COOKING TIME: 25 MINUTES

1 lb 2 oz boneless, skinless chicken breasts
1 egg yolk, lightly beaten
2 teaspoons soy sauce
2 teaspoons dry sherry
1/2 cup extra
2 1/2 tablespoons all-purpose flour
vegetable oil, for deep-frying
4 scallions, thinly sliced

LEMON SAUCE
1/3 cup lemon juice
2 tablespoons sugar
1 tablespoon dry sherry
2 teaspoons cornstarch

Cut the chicken into long strips, about 1 cm (1/2 inch) wide, and then set aside. Combine the egg, 1 tablespoon water, soy sauce, sherry and 3 teaspoons cornstarch in a small bowl and mix until smooth. Pour the egg mixture over the chicken, mixing well, and set aside for about 10 minutes.

Sift the remaining cornstarch and flour together onto a plate. Roll each piece of chicken in the flour, coating evenly, and shake off the excess. Place the chicken in a single layer on a plate.

Fill a wok one-third full of oil and heat to 350°F, or until a cube of bread dropped into the oil browns in 15 seconds. Carefully lower the chicken pieces into the oil, in batches, and cook for 2 minutes, or until golden brown. Remove the chicken with a slotted spoon and drain on paper towels. Repeat with the remaining chicken. Set aside while preparing the sauce. Reserve the oil in the wok.

To make the lemon sauce, combine 2 tablespoons water, the lemon juice, sugar, and sherry in a small saucepan. Bring to a boil over medium heat, stirring until the sugar dissolves. Stir the cornstarch into 1 tablespoon water and mix to a smooth paste, then add to the lemon juice mixture, stirring constantly until the sauce boils and thickens. Set aside.

Just before serving, reheat the oil in the wok to very hot, add all the chicken pieces and deep-fry for 2 minutes, or until very crisp and a rich golden brown. Remove the chicken with a slotted spoon and drain well on paper towels. Stack the chicken on a serving plate, drizzle over the sauce, sprinkle with the scallion and serve immediately.

NOTE: The first deep-frying of the chicken pieces can be done several hours in advance.

Tandoori Chicken with Cardamom Rice

❧ SERVES 4
❧ PREPARATION TIME: 15 MINUTES
❧ COOKING TIME: 45 MINUTES

1 cup Greek-style yogurt
¼ cup tandoori paste (see Note)
2 tablespoons lemon juice
4 cups cubed boneless, skinless chicken
   breasts
1 tablespoon oil
1 medium onion, finely diced
1½ cups long-grain rice
2 cardamom pods, bruised
3 cups hot chicken stock
9 cups baby spinach leaves
Greek-style yogurt, extra, to serve

Soak eight bamboo skewers in water for 30 minutes to prevent them burning during cooking.

Meanwhile, combine the yogurt, tandoori paste and lemon juice in a non-metallic dish. Add the chicken and coat well, then cover with plastic wrap and marinate for at least 10 minutes.

Heat the oil in a saucepan, add the onion and cook for 3 minutes, then add the rice and cardamom pods. Cook, stirring often, for 3–5 minutes, or until the rice is slightly opaque. Add the hot stock and bring to a boil. Reduce the heat to low, then cover and cook the rice, without removing the lid, for 15 minutes.

Meanwhile, wash the spinach and put it in a large saucepan with just the water clinging to the leaves. Cook, covered, over medium heat for 1–2 minutes, or until the spinach has wilted. Set aside and keep warm.

Preheat a barbecue plate or broiler to very hot. Thread the chicken cubes onto the soaked bamboo skewers, leaving the bottom quarter of the skewers empty. Cook the skewers on each side for 4–5 minutes, or until the chicken is cooked through.

Uncover the rice, fluff up with a fork and serve with the spinach, chicken and a dollop of extra yogurt.

NOTE: Tandoori paste is usually made up of a mixture of cumin, ground coriander, cinnamon, cloves, chili, ginger, garlic, turmeric, mace, salt, coloring and yogurt, though recipes do vary. There are many commercial varieties of paste available in jars from Indian grocery stores and large supermarkets.

Chicken and Almond Pilaff

⚜ SERVES 4–6

⚜ PREPARATION TIME: 15 MINUTES

⚜ COOKING TIME: 45 MINUTES

4 cups boneless, skinless chicken thighs,
    trimmed and cut into 1¼ inch wide
    strips
2 cups basmati rice
3 cups chicken stock
2 tablespoons ghee
1 large onion, chopped
1 medium garlic clove, finely chopped
1 teaspoon ground turmeric
1⅔ cups canned chopped tomatoes
1 cinnamon stick
4 cardamom pods, bruised
4 whole cloves
½ teaspoon finely grated lemon zest
3 tablespoons chopped cilantro leaves
2 teaspoons lemon juice
⅓ cup toasted slivered almonds

BAHARAT
1½ tablespoons coriander seeds
3 tablespoons black peppercorns
1½ tablespoons cassia bark
1½ tablespoons whole cloves
2 tablespoons cumin seeds
1 teaspoon cardamom seeds
2 whole nutmegs
3 tablespoons paprika

To make the baharat, grind the coriander seeds, peppercorns, cassia bark, cloves, cumin seeds and cardamom seeds to a powder using a mortar and pestle or in a spice grinder — you may need to do this in batches. Grate the nutmegs on the fine side of a grater and add to the spice mixture with the paprika. Stir together.

Combine the chicken and 1 tablespoon of the baharat in a large bowl, cover with plastic wrap and refrigerate for 1 hour. Meanwhile, put the rice in a large bowl, cover with cold water and soak for at least 30 minutes. Rinse under cold running water until the water runs clear, then drain and set aside.

Bring the stock to a boil in a saucepan. Reduce the heat, cover and keep at a low simmer. Meanwhile, heat the ghee in a large heavy-based saucepan over medium heat. Add the onion and garlic and cook for 5 minutes, or until soft and golden. Add the chicken and turmeric and cook for 5 minutes, or until browned. Add the rice and cook, stirring, for 2 minutes.

Add the chopped tomato, simmering chicken stock, cinnamon stick, cardamom pods, cloves, lemon zest and 1 teaspoon salt. Stir well and bring to a boil, then reduce the heat to low and cover the saucepan with a tight-fitting lid. Simmer for 20 minutes, or until the stock is absorbed and the rice is cooked. Remove from the heat and allow to stand, covered, for 10 minutes.

Stir in the cilantro, lemon juice and almonds. Season to taste.

NOTE: Baharat is an aromatic spice blend used in Arabic cuisine to add depth of flavor to dishes such as soups, fish curries and tomato sauces. Baharat can be stored in an airtight jar for up to 3 months in a cool, dry place. It can be used in Middle Eastern casseroles and stews, rubbed on fish that is to be broiled, pan-fried or barbecued, or used with salt as a spice rub for lamb roasts, cutlets or chops.

Curry Mee Noodles

❀ SERVES 4
❀ PREPARATION TIME: 30 MINUTES
❀ COOKING TIME: 30 MINUTES

2 large dried red chilies
1 teaspoon shrimp paste
14 oz egg noodles
1 onion, chopped
4 garlic cloves, chopped
4 lemon grass stems, white part only,
    thinly sliced
1 teaspoon grated fresh ginger
2 cups coconut cream
¼ cup Malaysian curry powder
14 oz boneless, skinless chicken thighs,
    thinly sliced
4¼ oz green beans, trimmed and cut into
    2 inch lengths
3 cups chicken stock
10 fried tofu puffs, halved diagonally
2 tablespoons fish sauce
2 teaspoons sugar
2 cups bean sprouts
2 hard-boiled eggs, quartered
2 tablespoons crisp-fried shallots
lime wedges, to serve

Soak the chilies in boiling water for 20 minutes. Drain, then chop. Wrap the shrimp paste in foil and put under a hot broiler for 1–2 minutes. Unwrap the shrimp paste.

Put the noodles in a bowl, cover with boiling water, and soak for 1 minute to separate. Rinse under cold water, drain and set aside.

Put the onion, garlic, lemon grass, ginger, chili, and shrimp paste in a food processor or blender and process to a rough paste, adding a little water if necessary.

Put 1 cup of the coconut cream in a wok and bring to a boil, then simmer for 10 minutes, or until the oil starts to separate from the cream. Stir in the paste and curry powder and cook for 5 minutes, or until fragrant. Add the chicken and beans and cook for 3–4 minutes, or until the chicken is almost cooked. Add the stock, tofu puffs, fish sauce, sugar, and the remaining coconut cream. Simmer, covered, over low heat for 10 minutes, or until the chicken is cooked.

Divide the noodles and bean sprouts among four bowls, then ladle the curry over the top. Garnish with the egg quarters and crisp fried shallots. Serve with the lime wedges.

Chicken Kapitan

✿ PREPARATION TIME: 35 MINUTES
✿ COOKING TIME: 30 MINUTES

1¹/₂ tablsspoons small dried shrimp
¹/₃ cup vegetable oil
4–8 red chilies, seeded and finely chopped
4 garlic cloves, finely chopped
3 lemon grass stems, white part only,
    finely chopped
2 teaspoons ground turmeric
10 candlenuts or macadamia nutes
2 large onions, chopped
1 cup coconut milk
1 lb 2 oz boneless, skinless, chicken thighs,
    chopped
¹/₂ cup coconut cream
2 tablespoons lime juice
steamed rice, to serve

Put the shrimp in a frying pan and dry-fry over low heat, shaking the pan regularly, for 3 minutes, or until the shrimp are dark orange and giving off a strong aroma. Transfer the shrimp to a mortar and pestle and pound until finely ground. Set aside.

Put half the oil with the chili, garlic, lemon grass, turmeric, and candlenuts in a food processor and process in short bursts until very finely chopped. Regularly scrape down the sides of the bowl with a rubber spatula.

Heat the remaining oil in a wok or frying pan, add the onion and ¹/₄ teaspoon salt, and cook over low heat for 8 minutes, or until golden, stirring regularly. Take care not to let the onion burn. Add the spice mixture and nearly all the ground shrimp, setting a little aside to use as garnish. Stir for 5 minutes. If the mixture begins to stick to the bottom of the pan, add 2 tablespoons coconut milk to the mixture. It is important to cook the mixture thoroughly to develop the flavors.

Add the chicken to the wok and stir well. Cook for 5 minutes, or until the chicken begins to brown. Stir in the remaining coconut milk and 1 cup water, and bring to a boil. Reduce the heat and simmer for 7 minutes, or until the chicken is cooked and the sauce is thick. Add the coconut cream and bring the mixture back to a boil, stirring constantly. Add the lime juice and serve immediately, sprinkled lightly with the reserved ground shrimp. Serve with steamed rice.

Chicken with Almonds and Asparagus

❀ SERVES 4–6
❀ PREPARATION TIME: 15 MINUTES
❀ COOKING TIME: 15 MINUTES

2 teaspoons cornstarch
1/3 cup chicken stock
1/4 teaspoon sesame oil
2 tablespoons oyster sauce
1 tablespoon soy sauce
3 garlic cloves, crushed
1 teaspoon finely chopped fresh ginger
pinch ground white pepper
2 1/2 tablespoons peanut oil
1/3 cup blanched almonds
2 scallions, cut into 1 1/4 inch lengths
1 lb 2 oz boneless, skinless chicken thighs,
    cut into thin pieces
1 small carrot, thinly sliced
5 1/2 oz asparagus, trimmed and cut into
    1 1/4 inch lengths
1/4 cup canned bamboo shoots, sliced
steamed rice, to serve

To make the stir-fry sauce, put the cornstarch and stock in a small bowl and mix to form a paste, then stir in the sesame oil, oyster sauce, soy sauce, garlic, ginger, and white pepper. Set aside until needed.

Heat a wok over high heat, add 2 teaspoons of the peanut oil and swirl to coat the base and side. Add the almonds and stir-fry for 1–2 minutes, or until golden — be careful not to burn them. Remove from the wok and drain on crumpled paper towels.

Heat another teaspoon of the peanut oil in the wok and swirl to coat. Add the scallion and stir-fry for 30 seconds, or until wilted. Remove from the wok and set aside.

Heat 1 tablespoon of the peanut oil in the wok over high heat, add the chicken in two batches, and stir-fry for 3 minutes, or until the chicken is just cooked through. Set aside.

Add the remaining peanut oil to the wok, then add the carrot and stir-fry for 1–2 minutes, or until just starting to brown. Toss in the asparagus and the bamboo shoots and stir-fry for a further 1 minute. Remove all the vegetables from the wok and set aside.

Stir the stir-fry sauce briefly, then pour into the wok, stirring until the mixture thickens. Return the chicken and vegetables to the wok and stir thoroughly for a couple of minutes until they are coated in the sauce and are heated through. Transfer to a serving dish and sprinkle with the almonds before serving. Serve with steamed rice.

Roast Chicken with Bacon and Sage Stuffing

❀ SERVES 6
❀ PREPARATION TIME: 15 MINUTES
❀ COOKING TIME: 1 HOUR 10 MINUTES

2 x 2 lb 12 oz whole chickens
6 bacon slices
2 tablespoons olive oil
1 small onion, finely chopped
1 tablespoon chopped sage
1 1/2 cups fresh breadcrumbs
1 egg, lightly beaten

WINE GRAVY
2 tablespoons all-purpose flour
2 teaspoons worcestershire sauce
2 tablespoons red or white wine
2 1/4 cups beef or chicken stock

Preheat the oven to 350°F. Remove the giblets and any large fat deposits from the chickens. Wipe over and pat dry inside and out with paper towels.

Finely chop two of the bacon slices. Heat half the oil in a small frying pan. Add the onion and the finely chopped bacon and cook until the onion is soft and the bacon is starting to brown. Transfer to a bowl and cool. Add the sage, breadcrumbs, and egg to the onion, season, to taste, and mix lightly. Spoon some stuffing into each chicken cavity.

Fold the wings back and tuck under the chickens. Tie the legs of each chicken together with string. Place the chickens on a rack in a large rosting pan, making sure they are not touching, and brush with some of the remaining oil. Pour 1 cup water into the pan.

Cut the remaining bacon into long, thin strips and lay across the chicken breasts. Brush the bacon with oil. Bake for 45–60 minutes, or until the juices run clear when a thigh is pierced with a skewer.

To make the gravy, discard all but 2 tablespoons of the pan juices from the raosting pan. Heat the dish on the stovetop over medium heat, add the flour and cook, stirring, until well browned. Remove from the heat and gradually add the worcestershire sauce, wine, and stock. Return to the heat, stir until the mixture boils and thickens, then simmer for 2 minutes. Season with salt and pepper, to taste.

Thai Green Chicken Curry

1 cup coconut cream
2¼ cups boneless, skinless chicken thighs,
    thinly sliced
1 cup sliced Chinese long beans
2 cups coconut milk
2½ cups small florets broccoli
1 tablespoon grated jaggery or unpacked
    brown sugar
2–3 tablespoons fish sauce
5 tablespoons cilantro leaves,
    plus extra, to garnish
steamed rice, to serve

CURRY PASTE
1 tablespoon shrimp paste
1 teaspoon coriander seeds, toasted
½ teaspoon cumin seeds, toasted
¼ teaspoon white peppercorns
5 cilantro stems
3 tablespoons chopped fresh galangal
10 long green chilies, chopped
1 medium lemongrass stem,
    white part only, chopped
6 medium red Asian shallots
3 medium garlic cloves
1 teaspoon grated lime zest
2 tablespoons peanut oil

To make the curry paste, preheat the broiler to high, wrap the shrimp paste in foil and put under the hot broiler for 5 minutes. Cool, remove the foil then put the shrimp paste in a food processor.

Put the coriander seeds, cumin seeds and peppercorns in a mortar and pestle and grind to a fine powder. Transfer to the food processor with ¼ teaspoon salt and the remaining paste ingredients. Blend until smooth.

Put the coconut cream in a wok over high heat, bring to a boil then simmer for 10 minutes, or until the oil starts to separate from the cream. Reduce the heat to medium. Stir in half the curry paste and cook for 2–3 minutes, or until fragrant. Add the chicken and cook for 3–4 minutes. Stir in the beans, coconut milk and broccoli. Bring to a boil then reduce the heat and simmer for 4–5 minutes, or until cooked. Stir in the sugar, fish sauce and cilantro leaves. Garnish with the extra cilantro and serve with steamed rice.

NOTE: Store the remaining curry paste in an airtight container in the refrigerator for up to 2 weeks.

Barbecued Chicken with Thai Sticky Rice

❧ SERVES 4–6
❧ PREPARATION TIME: 30 MINUTES
❧ COOKING TIME: 1 HOUR

4 lb 8 oz chicken, cut into 8–10 pieces
8 medium garlic cloves, chopped
6 cilantro stems, chopped
1 large handful cilantro leaves, chopped
1 tablespoon finely chopped fresh ginger
1 teaspoon ground white pepper
¼ cup fish sauce
¼ cup lime juice
¼ cup whiskey, optional
3 cups long-grain glutinous rice
cucumber slices, to serve

SAUCE
6 cilantro stems, chopped
4 medium garlic cloves, chopped
2 medium bird's eye chilies, seeded and
    chopped
¾ cup vinegar
4 tablespoons grated jaggery or soft
    brown sugar

Put the chicken pieces in a non-metallic bowl. Combine the garlic, cilantro stem and leaves, ginger, white pepper and a pinch of salt and pound to a paste using a mortar and pestle. Mix in the fish sauce, lime juice and whiskey (if desired), then pour over the chicken and mix well. Marinate for at least 6 hours in the refrigerator. At the same time, soak the rice for at least 3 hours in cold water.

To make the sauce, pound the cilantro stem, garlic, chili and a pinch of salt to a paste using a mortar and pestle. Combine the vinegar, jaggery and ¾ cup water in a saucepan and stir until the jaggery has dissolved. Bring to a boil, then add the paste and cook for 8–10 minutes, or until reduced by half. Set aside until ready to serve.

Drain the rice well, then line a bamboo steamer with muslin or banana leaves, spread the rice over and cover with a tight-fitting lid. Steam over a wok or large saucepan of boiling water for 40 minutes, or until the rice is translucent, sticky and tender. If steam is escaping, wrap some foil over the top of the steamer. Keep covered until ready to serve.

Meanwhile, heat a barbecue to medium heat, then cook the chicken, turning regularly for about 25 minutes, or until tender and cooked through. The breast pieces may only take about 15 minutes so take them off first and keep warm.

Serve the chicken, rice, dipping sauce and cucumber on separate plates in the center of the table and allow your guests to help themselves.

Thai Duck and Pineapple Curry

❀ SERVES 4–6
❀ PREPARATION TIME: 10 MINUTES
❀ COOKING TIME: 15 MINUTES

1 tablespoon peanut oil
8 medium scallions, sliced
    diagonally into 1¼ inch lengths
2 medium garlic cloves, crushed
2–4 tablespoons Thai red curry paste
4 cups chopped Chinese roast duck
1½ cups coconut milk
1¾ cups canned pineapple pieces in
    syrup, drained
3 kaffir lime leaves
3 tablespoons chopped cilantro leaves
2 tablespoons chopped mint

Heat a wok until very hot, add the oil and swirl to coat. Add the scallions, garlic and red curry paste, and stir-fry for 1 minute, or until fragrant.

Add the duck, coconut milk, pineapple pieces, kaffir lime leaves and half the cilantro and mint. Bring to a boil, then reduce the heat and simmer for 10 minutes, or until the duck is heated through and the sauce has thickened slightly. Stir in the remaining cilantro and mint, and serve with jasmine rice.

Duck Breast with Walnut and Pomegranate Sauce

❀ SERVES 4
❀ PREPARATION TIME: 15 MINUTES
❀ COOKING TIME: 25 MINUTES

4 large duck breasts
1 medium onion, finely chopped
1 cup fresh pomegranate juice
2 tablespoons lemon juice
2 tablespoons unpacked brown sugar
1 teaspoon ground cinnamon
1½ cups chopped walnuts
pomegranate seeds, to garnish, optional

Preheat the oven to 350°F. Score each duck breast two or three times on the skin side. Cook in a non-stick frying pan over high heat, skin side down, for 6 minutes, or until crisp and most of the fat has been rendered. Put in an ovenproof dish.

Remove all but 1 tablespoon of fat from the pan. Add the onion to the pan and cook over medium heat for 2–3 minutes, or until golden. Add the pomegranate juice, lemon juice, sugar, cinnamon and 1 cup of the walnuts and cook for 1 minute. Pour over the duck and bake for 15 minutes. Rest the duck for 5 minutes. Skim any excess fat from the sauce.

Slice the duck and serve with the sauce. Garnish with the pomegranate seeds and remaining walnuts.

Thai Duck and Pineapple Curry

Roast Pheasant

* SERVES 4–6
* PREPARATION TIME: 20 MINUTES
* COOKING TIME: 1 HOUR

2 x 2 lb 4 oz pheasants
6 thin bacon slices
8 medium sprigs thyme
2 large pieces of muslin
1/3 cup melted butter
2 medium apples, cored and cut into
   thick wedges
1/4 cup apple cider
1/2 cup whipping cream
2 teaspoons thyme leaves
2–4 teaspoons apple cider vinegar

Preheat the oven to 450°F. Rinse the pheasants and pat dry. Tuck the wings underneath the pheasants and tie the legs together with kitchen string. Wrap the bacon around each pheasant and secure with toothpicks. Thread the thyme sprigs through the bacon. Dip the pieces of muslin into the melted butter and wrap one around each pheasant.

Place on a rack in an ovenproof dish and bake for 10 minutes. Reduce the oven to 400°F and bake for a further 35 minutes. About 20 minutes before the end of the cooking, add the apple wedges to the base of the dish. The pheasants are cooked when the juices run clear when pierced with a skewer. Remove the pheasants and apple wedges, discard the muslin and toothpicks, then cover and keep warm.

Place the ovenproof dish with the juices on the stovetop. Pour the apple cider into the pan and bring to a boil. Cook for 3 minutes, or until reduced by half. Strain into a clean saucepan. Add the cream to the saucepan and boil for 5 minutes, or until the sauce thickens slightly. Stir in the thyme leaves and season well. Add the apple cider vinegar, to taste. Serve with the pheasant and apple.

Indonesian Spicy Chicken Soup

⚶ SERVES 6
⚶ PREPARATION TIME: 30 MINUTES
⚶ COOKING TIME: 2 HOURS

2 teaspoons coriander seeds
2 tablespoons vegetable oil
3 lb 2 oz whole chicken, jointed
   into 8 pieces
4 medium garlic cloves
1 medium onion, chopped
2 teaspoons finely sliced ginger
1 dried medium red chili, halved
2 medium lemongrass stems, white part
   only, roughly chopped
1 cup roughly chopped cilantro stems and
   stems, well rinsed
2 teaspoons ground turmeric
1 teaspoon galangal powder
1 teaspoon sugar
1 teaspoon ground coriander
4 cups chicken stock
2 tablespoons lemon juice
1¼ cups cellophane noodles
1½ tablespoons fish sauce
1 cup trimmed bean sprouts
3 tablespoons chopped cilantro leaves
4 medium scallions, thinly sliced
¼ cup crisp fried onions
1 tablespoon sambal oelek

Dry-fry the coriander seeds in a small frying pan over medium heat for 1 minute, or until fragrant. Cool, then finely grind using a mortar and pestle.

Heat a wok to very hot, add 2 teaspoons of the oil and swirl to coat the base and side. Add the chicken pieces and cook in batches for 3–4 minutes, or until browned all over. Remove from the wok and set aside.

Heat the remaining oil in the wok then add the garlic, onion, ginger and chili and stir-fry for 5 minutes, or until softened. Add the lemongrass, cilantro stem and stem, turmeric, galangal, sugar and ground coriander and cook for 5 minutes. Return the chicken to the wok and pour in the stock, lemon juice and 2 cups water to cover the chicken. Cover the wok with a lid and simmer for 20 minutes, skimming the surface periodically to remove any scum that rises to the surface. Remove only the chicken breast pieces, then cover the wok and simmer (still skimming the surface occasionally) for 20 minutes before removing the rest of the chicken pieces. Cover and refrigerate the chicken until needed. Return the lid to the wok and simmer the broth over low heat for 1 hour. Strain through a fine sieve, and allow to cool to room temperature before covering with plastic wrap and refrigerating overnight.

Soak the cellophane noodles in boiling water for 3–4 minutes then drain and rinse.

Remove any fat from the top of the cold broth. Remove the flesh from the chicken and shred with a fork. Place the broth and chicken flesh in the wok, and place over medium heat. Bring to a boil, then stir in the fish sauce, bean sprouts, cilantro leaves and noodles. Season well, then ladle into large bowls. Sprinkle with scallions and crisp fried onion, and serve with sambal oelek.

Clay Pot Chicken and Vegetables

❀ SERVES 4
❀ PREPARATION TIME: 20 MINUTES
❀ COOKING TIME: 25 MINUTES

1 lb 2 oz boneless, skinless
   chicken thighs
1 tablespoon soy sauce
1 tablespoon dry sherry
6 dried Chinese mushrooms
2 tablespoons peanut oil
2 small leeks, white part only, sliced
2 inch piece ginger, grated
1/2 cup chicken stock
1 teaspoon sesame oil
1²/₃ cups sliced sweet potato
3 teaspoons cornstarch
steamed rice, to serve

Wash the chicken under cold water and pat it dry with paper towel. Cut the chicken into small pieces. Put it in a dish with the soy sauce and sherry, cover and marinate for 30 minutes in the refrigerator.

Cover the mushrooms with hot water and soak for 20 minutes. Drain and squeeze to remove any excess liquid. Remove the stems and chop the caps into shreds.

Drain the chicken, reserving the marinade. Heat half the oil in a wok, swirling gently to coat the base and side. Add half the chicken pieces and stir-fry briefly until seared on all sides. Transfer the chicken to a flameproof clay pot or casserole dish. Stir-fry the remaining chicken and add it to the clay pot.

Heat the remaining oil in the wok. Add the leek and ginger and stir-fry for 1 minute. Add the mushrooms, remaining marinade, stock and sesame oil and cook for 2 minutes. Transfer to the clay pot with the sweet potato and cook, covered, on the top of the stove over very low heat for about 20 minutes.

Dissolve the cornstarch in a little water and add it to the pot. Cook, stirring over high heat, until the mixture boils and thickens. Serve the chicken and vegetables at once with steamed rice.

NOTE: Like all stews, this is best cooked 1–2 days ahead and stored, covered, in the refrigerator to allow the flavors to mature. It can also be frozen, but omit the sweet potato. Steam or boil the potato separately when the dish is reheating and stir it through.

Roast Duck with Rice Noodles

❧ SERVES 4–6
❧ PREPARATION TIME: 30 MINUTES
❧ COOKING TIME: 45 MINUTES

/2 oz dried Chinese mushrooms
1 1/2 oz wood ear fungus (see Note)
1 whole Chinese roast duck
1 tablespoon vegetable oil
2 teaspoons sesame oil
1 garlic clove, crushed
1 tablespoon grated fresh ginger
2/3 cup fresh baby corn, cut in half
    diagonally
2 scallions, thinly sliced
7 oz snow peas, cut in half diagonally
14 oz pak choy, cut into 3/4 inch lengths
3 1/2 fl oz oyster sauce
1 long red chili, seeded and finely sliced
5 cups chicken stock
1 tablespoon chopped cilantro leaves
1 tablespoon torn Thai basil
14 oz fresh rice noodle sheets, cut
        into 3/4 inch strips

Put the Chinese mushrooms in a heatproof bowl, cover with boiling water and soak for 30 minutes. Squeeze the mushrooms dry, discard the stems, and finely chop the caps. Put the wood ear fungus in a heatproof bowl, cover with boiling water and soak for 20 minutes, or until soft. Drain and cut into bite-sized pieces.

Remove the meat from the duck and thinly slice. Put the bones in a large saucepan with 96 fl oz (11 cups) water. Bring to a boil over high heat, then reduce the heat and simmer for 30 minutes. Remove any scum from the surface, then strain through a fine sieve.

Heat a wok over high heat, add the vegetable and sesame oils and swirl to coat the base and side. Add the garlic and ginger and fry for 30 seconds. Add the duck meat and stir-fry for 1 minute. Add the Chinese mushrooms, wood ear fungus, corn, scallion, snow peas, and bok choy and stir-fry for 2 minutes. Stir in the oyster sauce, chili, and stock and simmer for 2 minutes, or until heated through. Stir in the herbs.

Cover the noodles with boiling water and soak for 1–2 minutes, or until tender. Separate gently and drain. Divide among the bowls, then ladle the soup on top.

Note: Wood ear (also called black fungus) is a cultivated wood fungus. It is mainly available dried; it needs to be reconstituted in boiling water for a few minutes until it expands to five times its dried size, before cooking.

Japanese Udon Miso Soup with Chicken

❀ SERVES 4–6

❀ PREPARATION TIME: 35 MINUTES

❀ COOKING TIME: 10 MINUTES

8 dried shiitake mushrooms

1 cup boiling water

14 oz fresh udon noodles

4 cups chicken stock

1 lb 5 oz boneless, skinless chicken breast,
    cut into ⅝ inch thick strips

10½ oz baby pak choy, halved lengthways

¼ cup white miso paste

2 teaspoons dashi granules

1 tablespoon wakame flakes or other
    seaweed

5½ oz silken firm tofu, cut into
    ½ inch cubes

3 scallions, sliced diagonally

Soak the mushrooms in the boiling water for
20 minutes. Squeeze dry, reserving the soaking
liquid. Discard the woody stalks and thinly slice
the caps. Set aside.

Bring 8 cups water to a boil in a large saucepan and
cook the noodles for 1–2 minutes, or until tender. Drain
immediately and rinse under cold water. Set aside.

Pour the stock and 4 cups water into a wok and bring
to a boil, then reduce the heat and simmer. Add the
chicken and cook for 2–3 minutes, or until almost
cooked through.

Add the mushrooms and cook for 1 minute. Add the
bok choy halves and simmer for a further 1 minute, or
until beginning to wilt, then add the miso paste, dashi
granules, wakame, and reserved mushroom liquid. Stir
to dissolve the dashi and miso paste. Do not allow to boil.

Gently stir in the tofu. Distribute the noodles among the
serving bowls then ladle the hot soup over them.
Sprinkle with the scallions.

Kung Pao Chicken

☙ SERVES 4
☙ PREPARATION TIME: 15 MINUTES
☙ COOKING TIME: 10 MINUTES

1 egg white
2 teaspoons cornstarch
½ teaspoon sesame oil
2 teaspoons Chinese rice wine
1½ tablespoons soy sauce
2½ cups cubed boneless, skinless chicken
    thighs
¼ cup chicken stock
2 teaspoons Chinese black vinegar
1 teaspoon unpacked brown sugar
2 tablespoons vegetable oil
3 long dried red chilies, cut in half
    lengthways
3 medium garlic cloves, finely chopped
2 teaspoons finely grated fresh ginger
2 medium scallions, thinly sliced
⅓ cup roughly crushed unsalted raw
    peanuts

Lightly whisk together the egg white, cornstarch, sesame oil, rice wine and 2 teaspoons of the soy sauce in a large non-metallic bowl. Add the chicken and toss to coat in the marinade. Cover with plastic wrap and marinate in the refrigerator for 30 minutes.

To make the stir-fry sauce, combine the stock, vinegar, sugar and the remaining soy sauce in a small bowl.

Heat a wok over high heat, add 1 tablespoon of the vegetable oil and swirl to coat the base and side. Stir-fry the chicken in batches for about 3 minutes, or until browned. Remove from the wok.

Heat the remaining oil in the wok, then add the chili and cook for 15 seconds, or until it starts to change color. Add the garlic, ginger, scallions and peanuts and stir-fry for 1 minute. Return the chicken to the wok along with the stir-fry sauce and stir-fry for 3 minutes, or until heated through and the sauce has thickened slightly. Serve immediately.

NOTE: This dish is said to have been created for an important court official called Kung Pao (or Gong Bao), who was stationed in the Sichuan province of China. It is characterized by the flavors of the long, dried red chilies, popular in Sichuan cuisine, and the crunchiness of peanuts. It can also be made with meat or shrimp.

Braised Duck with Mushrooms

❊ SERVES 6
❊ PREPARATION TIME: 20 MINUTES
❊ COOKING TIME: 1 HOUR 10 MINUTES

2/3 cup dried Chinese mushrooms
3 lb 5 oz whole duck
2 teaspoons oil
2 tablespoons soy sauce
2 tablespoons Chinese rice wine
2 teaspoons sugar
2 wide strips orange peel
4 1/4 cups watercress

Soak the mushrooms in hot water for 20 minutes. Drain well, discard the stems and thinly slice the caps.

Using a large heavy knife or cleaver, chop the duck into small pieces, cutting through the bone. Arrange the pieces on a rack and pour boiling water over them — the water will plump up the skin and help keep the duck succulent. Drain and pat dry with paper towel.

Heat the oil in a wok over medium heat and add the duck. Cook, in batches, for about 8 minutes, turning regularly, until browned. (The darker the browning at this stage, the better the color when finished.) Between each batch, wipe out the pan with crumpled paper towel to remove excess oil.

Wipe the pan with paper towel again and return all the duck to the pan. Add the mushrooms, soy sauce, wine, sugar and orange peel. Bring the mixture to a boil, reduce the heat, cover and simmer gently for 35 minutes or until the duck is tender. Season to taste and stand for 10 minutes, covered, before serving.

Remove the duck from the sauce and discard the orange peel. Pick off small sprigs of the watercress and arrange them on one side of a large serving platter. Carefully place the duck segments on the other side of the plate — try not to place the duck on the watercress as it will become soggy. Carefully spoon a little of the sauce over the duck and serve.

NOTE: Braising the duck over low heat produces tender, melt-in-the-mouth meat and a delicious sauce. If the heat is too high, the duck will dry out and lose its flavor.

Roast Goose

❅ SERVES 6
❅ PREPARATION TIME: 15 MINUTES
❅ COOKING TIME: 1 HOUR 30 MINUTES

6 lb 12 oz whole goose

GRAVY
1 tablespoon all-purpose flour
2 tablespoons brandy
1 ½ cups chicken stock

BREAD SAUCE
1 small onion, sliced
1 ¼ cups milk
1 bay leaf
4 black peppercorns
2 whole cloves
1 ¼ cups fresh breadcrumbs
pinch freshly grated nutmeg
1 tablespoon butter

Preheat the oven to 350°F. Remove any excess fat from inside the cavity of the goose. Put the goose in a large roasting pan, cover with boiling water, then drain. Dry with paper towels. Put the goose, breast side down, on a rack in a very large roasting pan. Using a fine skewer, prick the skin of the goose all over. Bake for 1 hour, then remove from the oven and drain off any excess fat. Turn the goose over and bake for a further 30 minutes, or until golden. Remove from the baking dish, cover with foil, and leave for 5–10 minutes.

To make the gravy, drain all except 2 tablespoons of fat from the baking dish and put the dish on the stovetop over low heat. Add the flour and stir over medium heat until well browned. Gradually stir in the brandy and chicken stock. Stir until the gravy boils and thickens. Season.

To make the sauce, combine the onion, milk, bay leaf, peppercorns, and cloves in a saucepan. Bring to a boil over medium heat, then reduce the heat and simmer for 10 minutes. Strain into a bowl and discard the onion and flavorings. Add the breadcrumbs, nutmeg, and butter. Stir, then season.

Chicken Gumbo

🌺 SERVES 4–6
🌺 PREPARATION TIME: 15 MINUTES
🌺 COOKING TIME: 2 HOURS 30 MINUTES

1/3 cup vegetable oil
1/4 cup all-purpose flour
1 lb 5 oz boneless, skinless chicken thighs
1/4 cup unsalted butter
2/3 cup diced smoked ham
5 1/2 oz chorizo, thinly sliced
2 onions, chopped
2 garlic cloves, finely chopped
2 celery stalks, thinly sliced
1 redpepper, seeded, membrane removed,
    and finely chopped
1 lb tomatoes, peeled, seeded, and roughly
    chopped
2 cups chicken stock
1 bay leaf
2 teaspoons thyme
Tabasco sauce, to taste
12 oz okra, cut into 1/2 inch slices
2 scallions, sliced (optional)
2 tablespoons chopped Italian parsley
    (optional)

Heat 3 tablespoons of the oil in a small, heavy-based saucepan, add the flour and stir to make a smooth paste. Stir over very low heat for 1 hour, or until the roux turns very dark brown, but is not burnt. This requires a great deal of patience and stirring but provides the gumbo with its dark look and rich flavor — when it is done, the roux should be the color of dark chocolate. Remove from the heat.

Pat the chicken thighs dry with paper towels, cut into quarters and lightly season. Heat the remaining oil and half the butter in a heavy-based frying pan over medium heat. Cook the chicken for about 5 minutes, or until golden brown. Remove the chicken with a slotted spoon. Add the ham and chorizo and cook for 4–5 minutes, or until lightly golden. Remove, leaving as much rendered fat in the pan as possible.

Add the remaining butter to the same pan and cook the onion, garlic, celery, and pepper over medium heat for 5–6 minutes, or until the vegetables have softened but not browned. Transfer the vegetables to a heavy-based, flameproof casserole dish. Add the tomato and the roux to the vegetables and stir well. Gradually stir the stock into the pan. Add the herbs and season with the Tabasco. Bring to a boil, stirring constantly. Reduce the heat, add the chicken, ham and chorizo to the casserole dish and simmer, uncovered, for 1 hour. Add the okra and cook for 1 further hour. Skim the surface as the gumbo cooks because a lot of oil will come out of the chorizo. The gumbo should thicken considerably in the last 20 minutes as the okra softens. Remove the bay leaf and serve. Garnish with scallion and parsley, if desired.

NOTE: Gumbo is a speciality of Cajun cuisine and is a cross between a soup and a stew. Traditionally, gumbo is served in deep bowls, each containing a few tablespoons of cooked rice in the bottom.

Chicken and Chorizo Paella

※ SERVES 6
※ PREPARATION TIME: 30 MINUTES
※ COOKING TIME: 1 HOUR 5 MINUTES

1/4 cup olive oil
1 large red pepper, cut into 1/4 inch strips
2 1/2 cups cubed boneless, skinless chicken
    thighs
7 oz sliced chorizo
2 1/4 cups thinly sliced mushrooms
3 medium garlic cloves, crushed
1 tablespoon grated lemon zest
3 1/2 cups roughly chopped ripe medium
    tomatoes
1 2/3 cups trimmed green beans, cut into
    1 1/4 inch lengths
1 tablespoon chopped rosemary
2 tablespoons chopped Italian parsley
1/4 teaspoon saffron threads dissolved in
    1/4 cup hot water
2 cups short-grain white rice
3 cups hot chicken stock
6 lemon wedges, to serve

Heat the olive oil in a paella pan or in a large heavy-based, deep frying pan over medium heat. Add the red pepper strips and cook, stirring, for about 6 minutes, or until softened, then remove from the pan.

Add the chicken to the pan and cook for 10 minutes, or until browned. Remove from the pan. Add the chorizo to the pan and cook for 5 minutes, or until golden. Remove from the pan. Add the mushrooms, garlic and lemon zest to the pan, and cook over medium heat for 5 minutes.

Stir in the tomato and red pepper, and cook for a further 5 minutes, or until the tomato is soft.

Add the beans, rosemary, parsley, saffron mixture, rice, chicken and chorizo. Stir briefly and add the stock. Do not stir at this point. Reduce the heat and simmer for 30 minutes. Remove from the heat, cover and leave to stand for 10 minutes. Serve with lemon wedges.

NOTE: Paella pans are available from specialist kitchenware shops.

Butter Chicken

* SERVES 4–6
* PREPARATION TIME: 10 MINUTES
* COOKING TIME: 35 MINUTES

2 tablespoons peanut oil
2 lb 4 oz boneless, skinless chicken
    thighs, quartered
1/4 cup butter or ghee
2 teaspoons garam masala
2 teaspoons sweet paprika
2 teaspoons ground coriander
1 tablespoon finely chopped fresh ginger
1/4 teaspoon chili powder
1 cinnamon stick
6 cardamom pods, bruised
1 1/3 cups puréed tomatoes
1 tablespoon sugar
1/4 cup plain yogurt
1/2 cup whipping cream
1 tablespoon lemon juice

Heat a wok to very hot, add 1 tablespoon oil and swirl to coat the base and side. Add half the chicken and stir-fry for about 4 minutes, or until nicely browned. Remove from the wok. Add a little extra oil, if needed, and brown the remaining chicken. Remove from the wok and set aside.

Reduce the heat to medium, add the butter and stir until melted. Add the garam masala, paprika, ground coriander, ginger, chili powder, cinnamon stick and cardamom pods, and stir-fry for 1 minute, or until the spices are fragrant. Return the chicken to the wok and mix in until coated in the spices. Add the puréed tomatoes and sugar and simmer, stirring, for 15 minutes, or until the chicken is tender and the sauce is thick.

Stir in the yogurt, cream and lemon juice and simmer for 5 minutes, or until the sauce has thickened slightly.

Chicken Mulligatawny

☙ SERVES 6
☙ PREPARATION TIME: 25 MINUTES
☙ COOKING TIME: 4 HOURS

2 medium tomatoes, peeled
1 ⅓ tablespoons ghee
1 large onion, finely chopped
3 medium garlic cloves, crushed
8 curry leaves
¼ cup Madras curry paste
1 cup red lentils, washed and drained
⅓ cup short-grain rice
1 cup coconut cream
2 tablespoons chopped cilantro leaves
mango chutney, to serve

STOCK
3 lb 5 oz chicken
1 medium carrot, chopped
2 medium celery stalks, chopped
4 medium scallions, chopped
¾ inch piece ginger, sliced

To make the stock, put all the ingredients and 4 quarts cold water in a large stockpot or saucepan. Bring to a boil, removing any scum that rises to the surface. Reduce the heat to low and simmer, partly covered, for 3 hours. Continue to remove any scum from the surface. Carefully remove the chicken and cool. Strain the stock into a bowl and cool. Cover and refrigerate overnight. Discard the skin and bones from the chicken and shred the flesh into small pieces. Cover and refrigerate overnight.

Score a cross in the base of the tomatoes. Put in a heatproof bowl and cover with boiling water. Leave for 30 seconds then transfer to a bowl of cold water and peel the skin away from the cross. Cut the tomatoes in half, scoop out the seeds and chop the flesh.

Melt the ghee in a large saucepan over medium heat. Cook the onion for 5 minutes, or until softened but not browned. Add the garlic and curry leaves and cook for 1 minute. Add the curry paste, cook for 1 minute, then stir in the lentils. Pour in the stock and bring to a boil over high heat, removing any scum from the surface. Reduce the heat, add the tomato and simmer for 30 minutes, or until the lentils are soft.

Meanwhile, bring a large saucepan of water to a boil. Add the rice and cook for 12 minutes, stirring once or twice. Drain. Stir the rice into the soup with the chicken and coconut cream until warmed through — don't allow it to boil or it will curdle. Season. Sprinkle with the cilantro and serve with mango chutney.

Roast Chicken Stuffed with Pine Nuts and Rice

❦ SERVES 4–6

❦ PREPARATION TIME: 30 MINUTES

❦ COOKING TIME: 2 HOURS 30 MINUTES

STUFFING

1/4 cup clarified butter or ghee, melted
1 onion, chopped
1 teaspoon ground allspice
1/3 cup basmati rice
1/4 cup walnuts, chopped
1/3 cup pine nuts
1/3 cup golden raisins
1/2 cup chicken stock

3 lb 8 oz whole chicken
2/3 cup chicken stock

Preheat the oven to 350°F. Pour half the butter into a large frying pan, then add the onion and cook for 5 minutes over medium heat until the onion is transparent. Stir in the allspice.

Add the rice and nuts to the pan, then cook for 3–4 minutes over medium–high heat. Add the golden raisins, stock and 1/4 cup water. Bring to boil, then reduce the heat and simmer for 8–10 minutes, until the water is absorbed. Allow to cool.

Rinse the cavity of the chicken with cold water and pat dry inside and out with paper towels.

When the stuffing is cool, spoon it into the cavity. Truss the chicken, using string, then place in a deep baking dish, and rub 1/2 teaspoon salt and 1/4 teaspoon freshly ground black pepper into the skin, using your fingertips.

Pour the remainder of the butter over the chicken, then add the stock to the pan. Roast for 2 hours 10 minutes, basting every 20–25 minutes with juices from the pan. Rest the chicken for 15 minutes before carving. Serve with the stuffing.

Nonya Lime Chicken

❧ SERVES 4–6

❧ PREPARATION TIME: 20 MINUTES

❧ COOKING TIME: 25 MINUTES

CURRY PASTE

²/₃ cup red Asian shallots

4 garlic cloves

2 lemon grass stems, white part only,
   chopped

2 teaspoons finely chopped fresh galangal

1 teaspoon ground turmeric

2 tablespoons sambal oelek

1 tablespoon shrimp paste

¼ cup vegetable oil

2 lb 4 oz boneless, skinless chicken thighs,
   cut into 1¼ inch cubes

1²/₃ cups coconut milk

1 teaspoon finely grated lime zest

½ cup lime juice

6 kaffir lime leaves, finely shredded, plus
   extra, to garnish

2 tablespoons tamarind purée

steamed rice, to serve

lime wedges, to garnish

Combine the curry paste ingredients in a food processor or blender and blend until a smooth paste forms.

Heat a non-stick wok until very hot, add the oil, and swirl to coat the base and side. Add the curry paste and stir-fry for 1–2 minutes, or until fragrant. Add the chicken and stir-fry for 5 minutes, or until browned. Add the coconut milk, lime zest and juice, kaffit lime leaves and tamarind purée. Reduce the heat and simmer for 15 minutes, or until the chicken is cooked and the sauce has reduced and thickened slightly. Season well with salt. Serve with steamed rice and garnish with lime wedges and the extra kaffir lime leaves.

NOTE: 'Nonya' is an old Malaysian word which refers to a style fo cuisine which blends Chinese and Malaysian ingredients and cooking techniques — it is often spicy, harbaceous and aromatic.

meat

Peppered Beef Fillet with Béarnaise Sauce

❧ SERVES 6
❧ PREPARATION TIME: 30 MINUTES
❧ COOKING TIME: 45 MINUTES

2 lb 4 oz beef tenderloin
1 tablespoon oil
2 medium garlic cloves, crushed
1 tablespoon cracked black peppercorns
2 teaspoons crushed coriander seeds

BÉARNAISE SAUCE
3 medium scallions, chopped
1/2 cup dry white wine
2 tablespoons tarragon vinegar
1 tablespoon chopped tarragon
1/2 cup butter
4 egg yolks
1 tablespoon lemon juice

Preheat the oven to 425°F. Trim the fillet, removing any excess fat. Tie at regular intervals with kitchen string. Combine the oil and garlic, brush over the fillet, then roll the fillet in the combined peppercorns and coriander seeds.

Put the meat on a rack in an ovenproof dish. Bake for 10 minutes, then reduce the oven to 350°F and cook for a further 15–20 minutes for a rare result, or until cooked according to taste. Cover and leave for 10–15 minutes.

To make the béarnaise sauce, put the scallions, wine, vinegar and tarragon in a saucepan. Boil the mixture until only 2 tablespoons of the liquid remains. Strain and set aside. Melt the butter in a small saucepan. Place the wine mixture in a food processor with the egg yolks, and process for 30 seconds. With the motor running, add the butter in a thin stream, leaving the milky white sediment behind in the saucepan. Process until thickened. Add the lemon juice, to taste, and season.

Lamb Tagine with Quince

❧ SERVES 4–6
❧ PREPARATION TIME: 20 MINUTES
❧ COOKING TIME: 1 HOUR 40 MINUTES

3 lb 5 oz cubed lamb shoulder
2 large onions, diced
1/2 teaspoon ground ginger
1/2 teaspoon cayenne pepper
1/4 teaspoon crushed saffron threads
1 teaspoon ground coriander
1 cinnamon stick
1/2 cup roughly chopped cilantro leaves
2 2/3 tablespoons butter
1 lb 2 oz peeled, cored and quartered
　　quinces
1/2 cup dried apricots
cilantro sprigs, extra, to garnish

Place the lamb in a heavy-based flameproof casserole dish and add half the onion, the ginger, cayenne pepper, saffron, ground coriander, cinnamon stick, cilantro leaves and some salt and pepper. Cover with cold water and bring to a boil over medium heat. Reduce the heat and simmer, partly covered, for 1/2 hours, or until the lamb is tender.

While the lamb is cooking, melt the butter in a heavy-based frying pan and cook the remaining onion and the quinces for 15 minutes over medium heat, or until lightly golden.

When the lamb has been cooking for 1 hour, add the quinces and apricots and continue cooking.

Taste the sauce and adjust the seasoning if necessary. Transfer to a warm serving dish and sprinkle with cilantro sprigs. Serve with couscous or rice.

Pork Sausages with White Beans

❀ SERVES 4

❀ PREPARATION TIME: 25 MINUTES

❀ COOKING TIME: 1 HOUR 40 MINUTES

1¾ cups dried white beans

5½ oz tocino, speck or pancetta,
    unsliced

½ leek, white part only, thinly sliced

2 medium garlic cloves

1 medium bay leaf

1 small red chili, split and seeded

1 small onion

2 whole cloves

1 medium rosemary sprig

3 medium thyme sprigs

1 medium Italian parsley sprig

¼ cup olive oil

8 pork sausages

½ medium onion, finely chopped

1 medium green bell pepper, seeded and
    membrane removed, finely chopped

½ teaspoon paprika

½ cup puréed tomatoes

1 teaspoon cider vinegar

Soak the beans overnight in cold water. Drain and rinse the beans under cold water. Put them in a large saucepan with the tocino, leek, garlic, bay leaf and chili. Stud the onion with the cloves and add to the pan. Tie the rosemary, thyme and parsley together and add to the pan. Pour in 3 cups cold water and bring to a boil. Add 1 tablespoon of the oil, reduce the heat and simmer, covered, for 1 hour, or until the beans are tender. When necessary, add boiling water to keep the beans covered.

Prick each sausage five or six times and twist tightly in opposite directions in the middle to give two short fat sausages. Put in a single layer in a large frying pan and add enough cold water to reach halfway up their sides. Bring to a boil and simmer, turning a few times, until all the water has evaporated and the sausages brown lightly in the fat that is left in the pan. Remove from the pan and cut the short sausages apart. Add the remaining oil, the chopped onion and pepper to the pan and fry over medium heat for 5–6 minutes. Stir in the paprika, cook for 30 seconds, then add the puréed tomato and season. Cook, stirring, for 1 minute.

Remove the tocino, herb sprigs and any loose large pieces of onion from the bean mixture. Leave in any loose leaves from the herbs, and any small pieces of onion. Add the sausages and sauce to the pan and stir the vinegar through. Bring to a boil.

Red Cooked Pork Belly

❀ SERVES 6
❀ PREPARATION TIME: 10 MINUTES
❀ COOKING TIME: 2 HOURS 10 MINUTES

6 dried shiitake mushrooms
2 teaspoons peanut oil
2 lb 4 oz piece pork belly
2 cups chicken stock
$\frac{1}{4}$ cup dark soy sauce
$\frac{1}{4}$ cup Chinese rice wine
4 garlic cloves, bruised
2 inch piece fresh ginger, sliced
2 inch piece dried mandarin or tangerine
   peel
2 teaspoons sichuan peppercorns
2 star anise
1 cinnamon stick
$1\frac{1}{2}$ tablespoons Chinese rock sugar
   (see Note)
Thai basil sprigs, to garnish

Cover the mushrooms in 1 cup boiling water and soak for 20 minutes, or until soft. Squeeze dry, reserving the liquid.

Heat a large wok over high heat, add the oil, and swirl to coat. Add the pork, skin side down, and cook for 5 minutes, or until well browned, then turn over and cook for a further 6 minutes, or until sealed.

Add the stock, soy sauce, rice wine, garlic, ginger, citrus peel, spices, reserved mushroom soaking liquid, and 2 cups water. Bring to a boil, then reduce the heat to low and simmer, covered, for $1\frac{1}{4}$ hours.

Add the sugar and mushrooms and cook for a further 45 minutes, or until the pork is very tender. Remove the pork from the stock and cut into slices about $\frac{1}{2}$ inch thick. Strain the liquid into a bowl, then return the strained liquid to the wok. Bring to a boil and continue boiling until reduced to about $\frac{3}{4}$ cup.

Place the pork on a platter with the mushrooms and spoon on some of the cooking liquid. Garnish with the Thai basil. Serve with steamed rice.

NOTE: Chinese rock sugar is the crystallized form of saturated sugar liquor. It is named for its irregular rock-shaped pieces and imparts a rich flavor, especially to braised or 'red cooked' foods as well as sweets, glazing them with a translucent sheen. Available in the Asian section of large supermarkets, or in Asian grocery stores.

Surf 'n' Turf

❧ SERVES 4
❧ PREPARATION TIME: 20 MINUTES
❧ COOKING TIME: 15–20 MINUTES

1 large or 2 small raw lobster tails
2 tablespoons oil
4 x 7 oz beef tenderloin
1 cup fresh or frozen crabmeat
Italian parsley, to garnish

LEMON MUSTARD SAUCE
2 tablespoons butter
1 medium scallion, finely chopped
1 medium garlic clove, crushed
1 tablespoon all-purpose flour
1 cup whole milk
2 tablespoons whipping cream
1 tablespoon lemon juice
2 teaspoons dijon mustard

To make the sauce, melt the butter in a saucepan, add the scallion and garlic and stir over medium heat for 1 minute, or until the onion has softened. Stir in the flour and cook for 1 minute, or until pale and foaming. Remove from the heat and gradually stir in the milk. Return to the heat and stir constantly until the sauce boils and thickens. Reduce the heat and simmer for 2 minutes. Remove from the heat and stir in the cream, lemon juice and mustard. Keep warm.

Starting at the end where the head was, cut down each side of the lobster shell on the underside with kitchen scissors. Pull back the flap and remove the meat from the shell. Heat half the oil in a frying pan, add the lobster meat and cook over medium heat for 3 minutes each side (longer if using a large tail), or until just cooked through. Remove from the pan and keep warm. Reserve the oil in the pan.

Meanwhile, heat the remaining oil in a separate frying pan, add the steaks and cook over high heat for 2 minutes each side to seal, turning once. For rare steaks, cook each side 1 more minute. For medium and well-done steaks, reduce the heat to medium and continue cooking for 2–3 minutes each side for medium or 4–6 minutes each side for well-done. Remove from the pan and keep warm.

Add the crab to the reserved lobster pan and stir until heated through. To serve, place the steaks on plates. Top with crab followed by slices of lobster. Pour the sauce over the top and garnish with parsley.

Lamb Korma

❧ SERVES 4–6
❧ PREPARATION TIME: 30 MINUTES
❧ COOKING TIME: 1 HOUR

4 lb 8 oz leg of lamb, boned
1 onion, chopped
2 teaspoons grated fresh ginger
3 garlic cloves
1 tablespoon coriander seeds
2 teaspoons ground cumin
1 teaspoon cardamom pods
large pinch cayenne pepper
2 tablespoons ghee or vegetable oil
1 onion, extra, thinly sliced
2 tablespoons concentrated tomato purée
1/2 cup plain yogurt
scallions, sliced, to garnish
steamed rice, to serve

Remove all excess fat, skin, and sinew from the lamb. Cut the meat into 1 1/4 inch cubes and put in a large bowl.

Put the chopped onion, ginger, garlic, coriander seeds, cumin, cardamom pods, cayenne pepper and 1/2 teaspoon salt in a food processor and process until the mixture forms a smooth paste. Add the spice mixture to the lamb and mix well to coat. Set aside for 1 hour.

Heat the ghee or oil in a large frying pan. Add the sliced onion and cook, stirring, over medium–low heat until the onion is soft. Add the lamb mixture and cook for 8–10 minutes, stirring constantly, until the lamb is are browned all over. Add the tomato purée and 2 tablespoons of the yogurt, and stir until combined. Simmer, uncovered, until the liquid has been absorbed. Add the remaining yogurt, 2 tablespoons at a time, stirring until the mixture is nearly dry between each addition. Cover the pan and simmer over low heat for 30 minutes, or until the meat is tender, stirring occasionally. Add a little water if the mixture becomes too dry. Garnish with scallion and serve with steamed rice.

Rabbit with Rosemary and White Wine

❧ SERVES 4
❧ PREPARATION TIME: 25 MINUTES
❧ COOKING TIME: 2 HOURS

1 large rabbit (about 3 lb 8 oz)
1/4 cup seasoned flour
1/4 cup olive oil
2 medium onions, thinly sliced
1 large rosemary sprig
1 small sage sprig
2 medium garlic cloves, crushed
2 cups dry white wine
1 2/3 cups canned chopped tomatoes
good pinch of cayenne pepper
1/2 cup chicken stock
12 small black olives such as niçoise or
    ligurian, optional
3 small rosemary sprigs, extra

Cut the rabbit into large pieces and dredge the pieces in the flour. Heat the oil in a large heavy-based saucepan over heat. Brown the rabbit pieces on all sides, then remove from the saucepan.

Reduce the heat and add the onion, rosemary and sage to the saucepan. Cook gently for 10 minutes, then stir in the garlic and return the rabbit to the saucepan.

Increase the heat to high, add the wine to the pan and cook for 1 minute. Stir in the tomato, cayenne and half the stock. Reduce the heat, cover and simmer over low heat for about 1 1/2 hours, until the rabbit is tender. Halfway through cooking, check the sauce and if it seems too dry, add 1/4 cup water.

Discard the herb sprigs. If necessary, thicken the sauce by transferring the rabbit to a serving plate and cooking the sauce, uncovered, over high heat for about 5 minutes. Check the seasoning and adjust if necessary. Pour over the rabbit and garnish with the olives and extra rosemary. Polenta makes an excellent accompaniment to this dish.

Chinese Lamb, Garlic Chive and Cellophane Noodle Soup

※ SERVES 4
※ PREPARATION TIME: 10 MINUTES
※ COOKING TIME: 20 MINUTES

2 tablespoons light soy sauce
1 tablespoon oyster sauce
1 tablespoon Chinese rice wine
1 teaspoon sugar
1¼ teaspoons sesame oil
3 slices fresh ginger, plus 1 tablespoon
    finely chopped ginger, extra
9 oz lamb fillet
3½ oz cellophane noodles
1 tablespoon vegetable oil
2 scallions, finely chopped, plus extra,
    to serve
2 cups snipped garlic chives
4 cups chicken stock

Combine the soy sauce, oyster sauce, rice wine, sugar, ¼ teaspoon of the sesame oil, and the ginger slices in a bowl. Add the lamb and marinate for 3 hours, turning occasionally. Remove the lamb and ginger from the marinade with tongs. Set aside.

Meanwhile, soak the noodles in a bowl of boiling water for 3–4 minutes. Rinse, drain, and set aside.

Heat a wok over high heat, add the vegetable oil and the remaining sesame oil and swirl to coat the base and side. Add the chopped ginger, scallion, and garlic chives and cook for 30 seconds, stirring constantly. Slowly pour in the stock then bring to a boil. Add the lamb and ginger slices, reduce the heat to low, cover with a lid and poach the lamb for 10 minutes.

Remove the lamb from the wok. Bring the soup to a boil over medium heat. Meanwhile, thinly slice the lamb. Return the sliced lamb to the wok and add the noodles at the same time, stirring well until mixed together. Serve hot with the extra scallion scattered over the top.

Pork with Apple and Prune Stuffing

❀ SERVES 8

❀ PREPARATION TIME: 35 MINUTES

❀ COOKING TIME: 2 HOURS 10 MINUTES

1 medium granny smith apple, chopped
$1/3$ cup chopped pitted prunes
2 tablespoons port
1 tablespoon chopped Italian parsley
4 lb 8 oz piece boned pork loin
olive oil and salt, to rub on pork

GRAVY WITH WINE
2 tablespoons all-purpose flour
2 teaspoons worcestershire sauce
2 tablespoons red or white wine
$2^{1}/4$ cups beef or chicken stock

Preheat the oven to 475°F. To make the stuffing, combine the apple, prunes, port and parsley. Lay the pork loin on a board with the rind underneath. Spread the stuffing over the meat side of the loin, roll up and secure with skewers or string at regular intervals. If some of the filling falls out while tying, carefully push it back in. Score the pork rind with a sharp knife at $1/2$ inch intervals (if the butcher hasn't already done so) and rub generously with oil and salt.

Place on a rack in an ovenproof dish. Bake for 15 minutes, then reduce the heat to 350°F and bake for $1^{1}/2$–2 hours, or until the pork is cooked through. The juices will run clear when a skewer is inserted into the thickest part of the meat. Cover and stand for 15 minutes before removing the skewers or string and carving. Reserve any pan juices for making the gravy.

To make the gravy, discard all but 2 tablespoons of the pan juices from the ovenproof dish the roast was cooked in. Heat the dish on the stovetop over medium heat, stir in the flour and cook, stirring, until well browned. Remove from the heat and gradually add the worcestershire sauce, wine and stock. Return to the heat. Stir until the mixture boils and thickens, then simmer for 2 minutes. Season with salt and pepper, to taste.

NOTE: If the rind fails to crackle, carefully remove it from the meat, cutting between the fat layer and the meat. Scrape off any excess fat and put the rind on a piece of foil. Place under a hot broiler, and broil until the rind has crackled. Alternatively, place between several sheets of paper towel and microwave on High (100%) in 1 minute bursts, for about 2–3 minutes altogether (depending on the thickness of the rind).

Chinese Beef and Black Bean Sauce

❋ SERVES 4–6
❋ PREPARATION TIME: 15 MINUTES
❋ COOKING TIME: 20 MINUTES

2 tablespoons rinsed and drained black
   beans, chopped
1 tablespoon dark soy sauce
1 tablespoon Chinese rice wine
1 medium garlic clove, finely chopped
1 teaspoon sugar
1/4 cup peanut oil
1 medium onion, cut into wedges
1 lb 2 oz lean beef fillet, thinly
   sliced across the grain
1/2 teaspoon finely chopped fresh ginger
1 teaspoon cornstarch
1 teaspoon sesame oil
steamed rice, to serve

Put the beans, soy sauce, rice wine and 1/4 cup water in a small bowl and mix. In a separate bowl, crush the garlic and sugar to a paste, using a mortar and pestle.

Heat a wok over high heat, add 1 teaspoon of the peanut oil and swirl to coat the base and side. Add the onion and stir-fry for 1–2 minutes, then transfer to a bowl and set aside. Add 1 tablespoon of the peanut oil to the wok and swirl to coat the base and side, then add half the beef and stir-fry for 5–6 minutes, or until browned. Remove to the bowl with the onion. Repeat with the remaining beef.

Add the remaining peanut oil to the wok along with the garlic paste and ginger and stir-fry for 30 seconds, or until fragrant. Add the bean mixture, onion and beef. Bring to a boil, then reduce the heat and simmer, covered, for 2 minutes.

Combine the cornstarch with 1 tablespoon water, pour into the wok and stir until the sauce boils and thickens. Stir in the sesame oil and serve with steamed rice.

Veal Cooked with Vinegar

* SERVES 6–8
* PREPARATION TIME: 10 MINUTES
* COOKING TIME: 1 HOUR 50 MINUTES

½ cup all-purpose flour
large pinch cayenne pepper
2 lb 4 oz veal steaks
¼ cup olive oil
1 bay leaf
5 garlic cloves, crushed
⅔ cup red wine vinegar
2½ cups beef stock
chopped Italian parsley, to garnish

Combine the flour with the cayenne pepper and season well. Lightly coat the veal with the flour, shaking off any excess.

Heat the oil in a large, deep frying pan over high heat and cook the veal, a few pieces at a time, for 1 minute each side, or until lightly browned. Remove from the pan and set aside.

Add the bay leaf, garlic, red wine vinegar, and stock to the pan and bring to a boil, scraping up any residue from the base of the pan. Reduce the heat to low and return the veal and any juices back to the pan. Cover and cook, stirring occasionally, for 1½ hours, or until the veal is very tender and the sauce has thickened. If the sauce is too watery, carefully transfer the veal to a serving platter and boil the sauce until it is the consistency of a smooth gravy. Sprinkle with parsley before serving.

Roast Lamb with Lemon and Potatoes

* SERVES 6
* PREPARATION TIME: 20 MINUTES
* COOKING TIME: 3 HOURS

5 lb 8 oz–6 lb 12 oz leg of lamb
2 garlic cloves, thinly sliced
½ cup lemon juice
3 tablespoons dried oregano
1 onion, sliced
2 celery stalks, sliced
2 tablespoons butter, softened
2 lb 4 oz all-purpose potatoes, quartered

Preheat the oven to 350°F. Cut small slits in the lamb. Insert the garlic into the slits. Rub the entire surface with half the lemon juice, sprinkle with salt, pepper, and half the oregano. Place in a roasting pan and roast for 1 hour.

Drain the fat from the pan. Add the onion, celery and 1 cup hot water. Spread the butter over the lamb, reduce the oven to 325°F and cook for 1 hour. Turn during cooking to brown evenly.

Add the potatoes to the pan, sprinkle with the remaining oregano, lemon juice, and some salt and pepper. Bake for 1 hour, adding more water if required, and turning the potatoes halfway through cooking. Cut the lamb into slices. Skim any excess fat from the pan and serve the juices with the potatoes and lamb.

Veal Cooked with Vinegar

Thai Beef Curry

❀ SERVES 4

❀ PREPARATION TIME: 30 MINUTES

❀ COOKING TIME: 2 HOURS

1 tablespoon tamarind pulp

½ cup boiling water

2 tablespoons vegetable oil

3¾ cups cubed lean stewing beef

2 cups coconut milk

4 cardamom pods, bruised

2 cups coconut cream

2 tablespoons ready made Musaman
   curry paste

2 tablespoons fish sauce

8 pickling onions (see Notes)

8 baby potatoes (see Notes)

2 tablespoons grated jaggery or unpacked
   brown sugar

½ cup toasted and ground unsalted
   peanuts

Put the tamarind pulp and boiling water in a bowl and set aside to cool. Mash the pulp with your fingertips to dissolve the pulp, then strain and reserve the liquid, and discard the pulp.

Heat a non-stick wok over high heat, add the oil and swirl to coat the base and side. Add the beef in batches and cook over high heat for 5 minutes, or until browned all over. Reduce the heat, add the coconut milk and cardamom pods, and simmer for 1 hour, or until the beef is tender. Remove the beef from the wok. Strain the cooking liquid into a bowl and reserve.

Heat the coconut cream in the cleaned wok and stir in the curry paste. Cook for 10 minutes, or until the oil starts to separate from the cream. Add the fish sauce, onions, potatoes, beef mixture, jaggery, peanuts, tamarind water and the reserved cooking liquid. Simmer for about 30 minutes, or until the sauce has thickened and the meat is tender.

NOTES: It is important that the pickling onions and baby potatoes are small and similar in size to ensure that they cook evenly.
Also, use a non-stick or stainless-steel wok as the tamarind purée will react with the metal in a regular wok and badly taint the dish.

Pork Chops in Marsala

❧ SERVES 4
❧ PREPARATION TIME: 10 MINUTES
❧ COOKING TIME: 15 MINUTES

4 pork loin chops
2 tablespoons olive oil
1/2 cup Marsala
2 teaspoons grated orange zest
1/4 cup orange juice
3 tablespoons chopped Italian parsley

Pat dry the chops and season well. Heat the olive oil in a heavy-based frying pan over medium heat and cook the chops on both sides for 5 minutes each side, or until brown and cooked. Add the Marsala, orange zest, and juice and cook for 4–5 minutes, or until the sauce has reduced and thickened. Add the parsley and serve.

Shepherd's Pie

❧ SERVES 6
❧ PREPARATION TIME: 30 MINUTES
❧ COOKING TIME: 1 HOUR 15 MINUTES

1 tablespoon butter
2 onions, finely chopped
1/4 cup all-purpose flour
1/2 teaspoon dry mustard
1 1/2 cups chicken stock
1 lb 10 oz lean cooked roast lamb,
    trimmed of excess fat and finely
    chopped
2 tablespoons worcestershire sauce
4 large all-purpose potatoes
1/2 cup hot milk
1 1/2 tablspoons butter, extra

Lightly grease a 8-cup casserole dish. Preheat the oven to 425°F. Melt the butter in a large frying pan, add the onion and stir over medium heat for 5–10 minutes, or until golden. Add the flour and mustard to the pan and cook for 1 minute, or until pale and foaming. Remove from the heat and gradually stir in the stock. Return to the heat and stir until the sauce boils and thickens. Reduce the heat and simmer for 2 minutes. Add the meat and worcestershire sauce and stir. Season to taste. Remove from the heat and spoon into the casserole dish.

Steam or boil the potatoes for 10–15 minutes, or until just tender. Drain and mash well. Add the milk and butter to the mashed potato, season, and mix until smooth and creamy. Spread evenly over the meat and rough up the surface with the back of a spoon. Bake for 40–45 minutes, or until the meat is heated through and the topping is golden.

Pork Chops in Marsala

Game Pie

- SERVES 6–8
- PREPARATION TIME: 40 MINUTES
- COOKING TIME: 2 HOURS 30 MINUTES

2 lb 4 oz rabbit, boned, cut into bite-sized
   pieces
2 lb 12 oz diced venison
1/4 cup all-purpose flour
2–3 tablespoons olive oil
2 bacon slices, chopped
1 onion, sliced into thin wedges
2 garlic cloves, crushed
5 1/2 oz white mushrooms, halved
1 cup red wine
1 cup beef stock
3 thyme sprigs
2 bay leaves
6 1/2 oz ready-made puff pastry, thawed
1 egg yolk
2 tablespoons milk

Lightly coat the rabbit and venison in seasoned flour. Heat the oil in a large saucepan and cook the bacon over medium heat until golden. Remove. Brown the meat well in batches, remove, and set aside. Add the onion and garlic to the pan and cook until browned.

Return the bacon and meat to the pan and add the mushrooms, wine, stock, thyme, and bay leaves. Bring to a boil, then reduce the heat and simmer over low heat, stirring occasionally, for 1 1/2 hours, or until the meat is tender. Transfer to a heatproof bowl. Remove the thyme and bay leaves. Refrigerate until cold.

Preheat the oven to 400°F. Spoon the mixture into a 8-cup ovenproof dish. Roll out half the pastry on a lightly floured surface to about 1/4 inch thick. Cut strips the width of the pie dish rim, and secure to the dish with a little water. Reserve the leftover pastry. Roll out the other half of the pastry on a lightly floured surface until large enough to fit the top of the pie dish. Brush the edges of the pastry strips with a little combined egg yolk and milk. Drape the pastry over the rolling pin and lower it onto the top of the pie. Trim off any excess pastry using a sharp knife. Score the edges of the pastry with the back of a knife to seal. Use the leftover pastry to decorate the top. Cut two slits in the top of the pastry and brush all over with the remaining egg and milk mixture. Bake for 30–40 minutes, or until puffed and golden.

NOTES: Ask the butcher to bone the rabbit. Order the venison from the butcher.

Ramen Noodle Soup with Barbecued Pork and Greens

$^1/_2$ oz dried shiitake mushrooms
$^1/_2$ cup boiling water
12 oz gai larn, trimmed and cut into
    1$^1/_2$ inch lengths
13 oz fresh ramen noodles
5 cups chicken stock
$^1/_4$ cup soy sauce
1 teaspoon sugar
7 oz Chinese barbecued pork (char siu),
    thinly sliced
chili flakes (optional)

Soak the mushrooms in the boiling water for 20 minutes. Squeeze the mushrooms dry, reserving the liquid. Discard the stalks, then thinly slice the caps. Set aside.

Blanch the Chinese broccoli in a large saucepan of boiling salted water for 3 minutes, or until tender but firm to the bite. Drain, then refresh in cold water. Set aside.

Cook the noodles in a large saucepan of boiling water for 2 minutes, or until just tender. Drain, rinse under cold water, then drain again. Set aside.

Pour the stock and 2 cups water into a non-stick wok and bring to a boil. Add the sliced mushrooms and reserved mushroom liquid, soy sauce, and sugar. Simmer for 2 minutes, then add the broccoli.

Divide the noodles among four serving bowls. Ladle on the hot stock and vegetables. Top with the pork and chili flakes, if desired.

Mexican Beef Chili with Beans and Rice

❧ SERVES 4–6
❧ PREPARATION TIME: 20 MINUTES
❧ COOKING TIME: 2 HOURS

2 cups long-grain white rice
2 tablespoons olive oil
1 lb 5 oz chuck steak, cut into ¾ inch
    cubes
1 medium red onion, chopped
3 medium garlic cloves, crushed
1 long green chili, finely chopped
2½ teaspoons ground cumin
2 teaspoons ground coriander
1 teaspoon chili powder
3 teaspoons dried oregano
1²⁄₃ cups canned chopped tomatoes
2 tablespoons concentrated tomato purée
3 cups beef stock
1½ cups canned kidney beans, drained
    and rinsed
2 tablespoons oregano, chopped
burritos, to serve
sour cream, to serve

Put the rice in a heatproof bowl, add enough boiling water to cover it and leave it to soak until cool.

Meanwhile, heat 1 tablespoon of the oil in a large heavy-based saucepan. Cook the beef in two batches until browned, then remove from the pan.

Heat the remaining oil in the pan and cook the onion for 2 minutes, or until softened but not browned. Add the garlic and chili and cook for a further minute, then add the cumin, ground coriander, chili powder and dried oregano and cook for a further 30 seconds. Return the beef to the pan and add the chopped tomato, concentrated tomato purée and 1 cup of the stock. Bring to a boil, then reduce the heat and simmer, covered, for 1½ hours, or until the beef is tender.

Drain the rice and stir it into the beef mixture along with the kidney beans and remaining stock. Bring the mixture to a boil, then reduce the heat and simmer, covered, for 20 minutes, or until the rice is tender and all the liquid has been absorbed. Stir in the oregano and serve with warmed burritos and a dollop of sour cream. Let your guests assemble their own burritos at the table.

Rack of Lamb with Herb Crust

※ SERVES 4
※ PREPARATION TIME: 25 MINUTES
※ COOKING TIME: 25 MINUTES

2 x 6–rib racks of lamb, French trimmed
1 tablespoon oil
1 cup fresh breadcrumbs
3 medium garlic cloves
3 tablespoons finely chopped Italian
    parsley
2 teaspoons thyme leaves
1/2 teaspoon finely grated lemon zest
1/4 cup softened butter
1 cup beef stock
1 medium garlic clove, extra,
    finely chopped
1 medium thyme sprig

Preheat the oven to 500°F. Score the fat on the lamb racks in a diamond pattern. Rub with a little oil and season.

Heat the oil in a frying pan over high heat, add the lamb racks and brown for 4–5 minutes. Remove and set aside. Do not wash the pan as you will need it later.

In a large bowl, mix the breadcrumbs, garlic, parsley, thyme leaves and lemon zest. Season, then mix in the butter to form a paste.

Firmly press a layer of breadcrumb mixture over the fat on the lamb racks, leaving the bones and base clean. Bake in a roasting pan for 12 minutes for medium-rare. Rest the lamb on a plate while you make the jus.

To make the jus, add the beef stock, extra garlic and thyme sprig to the roasting pan juices, scraping the pan. Return this liquid to the original frying pan and simmer over high heat for 5–8 minutes, or until the sauce has reduced. Strain and serve with the lamb.

Harira

2 tablespoons olive oil
2 small brown onions, chopped
2 large garlic cloves, crushed
1 lb 2 oz lamb shoulder steaks, trimmed of
    excess fat and sinew, and cut into small
    chunks
1½ teaspoons ground cumin
2 teaspoons paprika
½ teaspoon ground cloves
1 bay leaf
2 tablespoons concentrated tomato purée
4 cups beef stock
2 lb canned chickpeas, rinsed and drained
3¼ cups canned diced tomatoes
¾ cup finely chopped cilantro leaves,
    plus extra, to garnish
small niçoise olives, to serve

Heat the oil in a large heavy-based saucepan or stockpot, add the onion and garlic, and cook for 5 minutes, or until softened. Add the meat in batches and cook over high heat until browned on all sides. Return all the meat to the pan.

Add the spices and bay leaf to the pan and cook until fragrant. Add the tomato purée and cook for about 2 minutes, stirring constantly. Add the stock, stir well, and bring to a boil. Add the chickpeas, tomatoes, and the chopped cilantro to the pan. Stir, then bring to a boil. Reduce the heat and simmer for 2 hours, or until the meat is tender. Stir occasionally. Season to taste.

Serve garnished with cilantro leaves and olives. This dish can also be served with toasted pita bread drizzled with a little extra virgin olive oil.

Beef Pho

❄ SERVES 4
❄ PREPARATION TIME: 15 MINUTES
❄ COOKING TIME: 35 MINUTES

8 cups beef stock

1 star anise

1½ inch piece fresh ginger, sliced

2 pigs' trotters, halved

½ onion, studded with 2 whole cloves

2 lemon grass stems, white part only,
   bruised

2 garlic cloves, crushed

¼ teaspoon ground white pepper

1 tablespoon fish sauce, plus extra, to serve

7 oz fresh thin rice noodles

10½ oz beef fillet, partially frozen, thinly
   sliced

1 cup bean sprouts, trimmed

2 scallions, thinly sliced,

¾ cup chopped cilantro leaves, plus extra,
   to serve

4 tablespoons chopped Vietnamese mint,
   plus extra, to serve

1 red chili, thinly sliced, plus extra, to serve

2 limes, quartered

Put the beef stock, star anise, ginger, pigs' trotters, onion, lemon grass, garlic, and white pepper in a wok and bring to a boil. Reduce the heat to very low and simmer, covered, for 30 minutes. Strain, return to the wok, and stir in the fish sauce.

Meanwhile, put the noodles in a heatproof bowl, cover with boiling water and gently separate. Drain well, then refresh under cold running water. Divide the noodles among four deep soup bowls then top with beef strips, bean sprouts, scallion, cilantro, mint, and chili. Ladle over the broth

Place the extra chili, mint, cilantro, lime quarters, and fish sauce in small bowls on a platter, serve with the soup and allow guests to help themselves.

Roman Lamb

※ SERVES 4–6
※ PREPARATION TIME: 15 MINUTES
※ COOKING TIME: 1 HOUR 20 MINUTES

¼ cup olive oil
2 lb 4 oz spring lamb, cut into ¾ inch
    cubes
2 garlic cloves, crushed
6 sage leaves
1 rosemary sprig
1 tablespoon all-purpose flour
½ cup white wine vinegar
6 anchovy fillets

Heat the oil in a heavy-based frying pan and cook the meat in batches over medium heat for 3–4 minutes, until brown on all sides. Return all the meat to the pan and add the garlic, sage, and rosemary. Season, combine well, and cook for 1 minute.

Dust the meat with the flour using a fine sieve, then cook for a further 1 minute. Add the vinegar and simmer for 30 seconds, then add 250 ml 1 cup water. Bring to a gentle simmer, lower the heat and cover, leaving the lid partially askew. Cook for 50–60 minutes, or until the meat is tender, stirring occasionally, and adding a little more water if necessary.

When the lamb is almost cooked, mash the anchovies and 1 tablespoon of the cooking liquid to a paste using a mortar and pestle. Add to the lamb and cook, uncovered, for another 2 minutes.

Chili Plum Beef

※ SERVES 4
※ PREPARATION TIME: 15 MINUTES
※ COOKING TIME: 15 MINUTES

2 tablespoons vegetable oil
1 lb 5 oz lean beef fillet, thinly sliced
    across the grain
1 large red onion, cut into wedges
1 red pepper, seeded, membrane removed,
    and finely sliced
1½ tablespoons chili garlic sauce
½ cup plum sauce
1 tablespoon light soy sauce
2 teaspoons rice vinegar
pinch finely ground white pepper
4 scallions, sliced
steamed rice or noodles, to serve

Heat a wok over high heat, add 1 tablespoon of the oil and swirl to coat the base and side. Stir-fry the beef in two batches for 2–3 minutes, or until browned and just cooked. Remove from the wok and set aside.

Heat the remaining oil in the wok, add the onion and stir-fry for 1 minute, then add the pepper and stir-fry for 2–3 minutes, or until just tender. Add the chili garlic sauce and stir for 1 minute, then return the meat to the wok and add the plum sauce, soy sauce, vinegar, white pepper, and most of the scallion.

Toss everything together for 1 minute, or until the meat is heated through. Sprinkle with the remaining scallion and serve with steamed rice or noodles.

Roman Lamb

Rigatoni with Italian-style Oxtail Sauce

❀ SERVES 4
❀ PREPARATION TIME: 25 MINUTES
❀ COOKING TIME: 2 HOURS

2 tablespoons olive oil
3 lb 5 oz oxtail, jointed
2 large onions, sliced
4 medium garlic cloves, chopped
2 medium celery stalks, sliced
2 medium carrots, thinly sliced
2 large rosemary sprigs
1/4 cup red wine
1/4 cup concentrated tomato purée
4 medium tomatoes, peeled and chopped
6 cups beef stock
7 1/2 cups rigatoni

Heat the oil in a large heavy-based saucepan. Brown the oxtail, remove from the pan and set aside. Add the onion, garlic, celery and carrot to the pan and stir for 3–4 minutes, or until the onion is lightly browned.

Return the oxtail to the pan and add the rosemary and red wine. Cover and cook for 10 minutes, shaking the pan occasionally to prevent the meat from sticking to the bottom. Add the concentrated tomato purée and chopped tomato to the pan with 2 cups of the beef stock and simmer, uncovered, for 30 minutes, stirring the mixture occasionally.

Add another 2 cups of beef stock to the pan and cook for 30 minutes. Add 1 cup of stock and cook for 30 minutes. Finally, add the remaining stock and cook until the oxtail is tender and the meat is falling from the bone. The liquid should have reduced to produce a thick sauce.

Just before the meat is cooked, cook the pasta in a large saucepan of rapidly boiling salted water until *al dente*. Serve the meat and sauce over the hot pasta.

NOTE: For a different flavor, you can add 9 oz bacon to the cooked onion, garlic and vegetables.

Beef Wellington

* SERVES 6–8
* PREPARATION TIME: 25 MINUTES
* COOKING TIME: 1 HOUR 30 MINUTES

2 lb 12 oz beef fillet or rib-eye in 1 piece
1 tablespoon oil
½ cup pâté
⅔ cup sliced white mushrooms
2 sheets frozen puff pastry, thawed
1 egg, lightly beaten
1 sheet frozen puff pastry, thawed

Preheat the oven to 425°F. Trim the meat of any excess fat and sinew. Fold the thinner part of the tail end under the meat and tie securely with kitchen string at regular intervals to form an even shape.

Rub the meat with freshly ground black pepper. Heat the oil over high heat in a large frying pan. Add the meat and brown well all over. Remove from the heat and allow to cool. Remove the string.

Spread the pâté over the top and sides of the beef. Cover with the mushrooms, pressing them onto the pâté. Roll out the block pastry on a lightly floured surface to a rectangle large enough to completely enclose the beef.

Place the beef on the pastry, brush the edges with egg, and fold over to enclose the meat completely, brushing the edges of the pastry with the beaten egg to seal, and folding in the ends. Invert onto a greased baking sheet so the seam is underneath. Cut leaf shapes from the sheet of puff pastry and use to decorate the Wellington. Use the egg to stick on the shapes. Cut a few slits in the top to allow the steam to escape. Brush the top and sides of the pastry with egg, and cook for 45 minutes for rare, 1 hour for medium or 1½ hours for well-done. Leave in a warm place for 10 minutes before cutting into slices for serving.

NOTE: Use a firm pâté, discarding any jelly. Cover the pastry loosely with foil if it begins to darken too much.

Stuffed Leg of Lamb

※ SERVES 6–8
※ PREPARATION TIME: 25 MINUTES
※ COOKING TIME: 2 HOURS 15 MINUTES

1 large leg of lamb (6 lb 12 oz), boned
1 teaspoon sweet paprika
1 tablespoon all-purpose flour
4 medium garlic cloves, peeled
2 tablespoons olive oil
1½ cups dry white wine
1 tablespoon lard
½ cup chicken stock

STUFFING
1 thick slice white bread, crusts removed
2½ oz chicken livers, trimmed
⅓ cup tocino or bacon
1 tablespoon dry sherry
1 medium garlic clove, crushed
1 tablespoon chopped Italian parsley
½ tablespoon chopped chives
1 teaspoon finely chopped rosemary
1 tablespoon capers, finely chopped

To make the stuffing, break the bread into pieces and process with the chicken livers and tocino until medium-fine. Put in a bowl with the sherry, garlic, parsley, chives, rosemary and capers. Season and mix well.

Preheat the oven to 425°F. Lay the lamb out flat and put the filling down the center. Roll the meat up to encase the filling. Tie with kitchen string. Combine the paprika and flour with ¼ teaspoon salt and rub all over the lamb. Put the garlic in a row in the center of an ovenproof dish and pour the oil over the top. Put the lamb on the garlic and pour the wine over the top. Spread the lard over the surface.

Bake for 20 minutes, then reduce the heat to 325°F. Baste, then bake for a further 1 hour 45 minutes, basting frequently, until the lamb is well cooked. Transfer to a carving tray and keep warm. Spoon off excess oil from the pan juices, then transfer the contents of the ovenproof dish to a saucepan; there will be about ½ cup. Add the stock and cook over high heat until slightly thickened. Slice the lamb and arrange on a serving platter. Pour the sauce over the lamb.

Parmesan and Rosemary Crusted Veal Chops

❧ SERVES 4
❧ PREPARATION TIME: 15 MINUTES
❧ COOKING TIME: 15 MINUTES

4 veal chops
1 3/4 cup fresh white breadcrumbs
3/4 cup freshly grated parmesan cheese
1 tablespoon rosemary, finely chopped
2 eggs, lightly beaten, seasoned
1/4 cup olive oil
1/4 cup butter
4 medium garlic cloves

Trim the chops of excess fat and sinew and flatten to 1/2 inch thickness. Pat the meat dry with paper towels. Combine the breadcrumbs, parmesan and rosemary in a shallow bowl.

Dip each chop in the beaten egg, draining off excess. Press both sides of the chops firmly in the crumbs.

Heat the oil and butter in a heavy-based frying pan over low heat, add the garlic and cook until golden. Discard the garlic.

Increase the heat to medium, add the chops to the pan and cook for 4–5 minutes on each side, depending on the thickness of the chops, until golden and crisp. Transfer to a warm serving dish and season.

Spaghetti Bolognese

❧ SERVES 4–6
❧ PREPARATION TIME: 20 MINUTES
❧ COOKING TIME: 1 HOUR 40 MINUTES

2 tablespoons olive oil
2 garlic cloves, crushed
1 large onion, chopped
1 carrot, chopped
1 celery stalk, chopped
1 lb 2 oz ground beef
2 cups beef stock
1 1/2 cups red wine
3 1/2 cups canned crushed tomatoes
1 teaspoon sugar
3 tablespoons chopped Italian parsley
1 lb 2 oz spaghetti
freshly grated parmesan cheese, to serve

Heat the olive oil in a large deep frying pan. Add the garlic, onion, carrot, and celery and stir for 5 minutes over low heat until the vegetables are golden.

Increase the heat, add the beef and brown well, stirring and breaking up any lumps with a fork as it cooks. Add the stock, wine, tomatoes, sugar, and parsley.Bring the mixture to a boil, reduce the heat and simmer for 1 1/2 hours, stirring occasionally. Season to taste.

While the sauce is cooking and shortly before serving, cook the pasta in a large saucepan of rapidly boiling salted water until *al dente*. Drain and then divide among serving bowls. Serve the sauce over the top of the pasta and sprinkle with the freshly grated parmesan cheese.

Parmesan and Rosemary Crusted Veal Chops

Steak and Kidney Pie

⚹ SERVES 6
⚹ PREPARATION TIME: 20 MINUTES
⚹ COOKING TIME: 1 HOUR 50 MINUTES

1 lb 10 oz round steak, trimmed of
   excess fat and sinew
4 lamb kidneys
2 tablespoons all-purpose flour
1 tablespoon oil
1 medium onion, chopped
2 tablespoons butter
1 tablespoon worcestershire sauce
1 tablespoon concentrated tomato purée
$\frac{1}{2}$ cup red wine
1 cup beef stock
$1\frac{1}{3}$ cups sliced white mushrooms
$\frac{1}{2}$ teaspoon dried thyme
4 tablespoons chopped Italian parsley
2 sheets frozen puff pastry, thawed
1 egg, lightly beaten

Cut the steak into $^3/_4$ inch cubes. Peel the skin from the kidneys, quarter them and trim away any fat or sinew. Put the flour in a plastic bag with the meat and kidneys and toss gently. Heat the oil in a frying pan, add the onion and fry for 5 minutes, or until soft. Remove from the pan with a slotted spoon. Add the butter to the pan, brown the steak and kidneys in batches and then return the steak, kidneys and onion to the pan.

Add the worcestershire sauce, concentrated tomato purée, wine, stock, mushrooms and herbs to the pan. Bring to a boil, reduce the heat and simmer, covered, for 1 hour, or until the meat is tender. Season to taste and allow to cool. Spoon into a 6-cup pie dish.

25°F. Roll the pastry between two sheets of parchment paper, to a size $1\frac{1}{2}$ inches larger than the pie dish. Cut thin strips from the edge of the pastry and press onto the rim of the dish, sealing the joins. Place the pastry on the pie, trim the edges and cut two steam holes in the pastry. Decorate the pie with leftover pastry and brush the top with egg. Bake for 35–40 minutes, or until the pastry is golden.

Veal Wrapped in Prosciutto with Honeyed Wild Rice

※ SERVES 4
※ PREPARATION TIME: 25 MINUTES
※ COOKING TIME: 35 MINUTES

1 lb 2 oz spinach, stalks removed
4 x 7 oz veal steaks, slightly flattened
16 slices prosciutto
2 tablespoons wholegrain mustard

HONEYED WILD RICE
1 cup wild rice blend
1½ tablespoons butter
1 onion, finely chopped
1 garlic clove, crushed
1 tablespoon honey
1 tablespoon light soy sauce

2 tablespoons olive oil
2 garlic cloves, crushed
½ cup dry white wine
1 cup chicken stock
1 tablespoon dijon mustard
1 teaspoon cornstarch, blended with
    2 tablespoons cold water
1 tablespoon chervil sprigs

Preheat the oven to 350°F. Steam the spinach until just wilted, then rinse in cold water, drain and pat dry. Put a few spinach leaves on a cutting board to form a square, a little larger than a veal steak. Also on the board, lay out four prosciutto slices, slightly overlapping, with the short ends towards you. Put a steak on the spinach square, spread it with a quarter of the wholegrain mustard and roll up both the veal and spinach to form a log. Lay the veal and spinach log across the bottom edge of the pieces of prosciutto and roll up, folding in the sides as you go, to form a parcel. Repeat with the remaining spinach, veal, wholegrain mustard, and prosciutto until you end up with four parcels.

To make the honeyed wild rice, bring a large saucepan of water to a boil. Add the rice and cook, stirring occasionally, for 25 minutes, or until tender, then drain. Heat the butter in a small frying pan, add the onion and garlic, and cook until the onion is softened but not browned. Add the rice, honey, and soy sauce, toss thoroughly, then remove from the heat.

Meanwhile, heat the oil in a frying pan over medium heat and cook the veal parcels until lightly browned, turning frequently. Remove from the pan and transfer to a roasting pan. Bake for 10–15 minutes. Remove from the oven, cover, and keep warm.

Put the roasting pan on the stovetop over medium heat, add the garlic and wine and cook for 2 minutes. Add the stock, dijon mustard, and cornstarch paste. Stir until the sauce boils and thickens. Strain. Slice the veal thickly, pour over the sauce and sprinkle with the chervil.

Saltimbocca

❧ SERVES 4

❧ PREPARATION TIME: 15 MINUTES

❧ COOKING TIME: 20 MINUTES

4 thin veal steaks
2 medium garlic cloves, crushed
4 medium prosciutto slices
4 sage leaves
2 tablespoons butter
$2/3$ cup Marsala

Trim the meat of excess fat and sinew and flatten each steak to $1/4$ inch thick. Nick the edges to prevent curling and pat the meat dry with paper towels. Combine the garlic with $1/4$ teaspoon salt and $1/2$ teaspoon ground black pepper and rub some of the mixture over one side of each veal steak. Place a slice of prosciutto on each and top with a sage leaf. The prosciutto should cover the veal completely but not overlap the edge.

Melt the butter in a large heavy-based frying pan, add the veal, prosciutto side up, and cook over heat for 5 minutes, or until the underside is golden brown. Do not turn the veal. Add the Marsala, without wetting the top of the veal. Reduce the heat and simmer very slowly for 10 minutes. Transfer the veal to warm serving plates. Boil the sauce for 2–3 minutes, or until syrupy, then spoon it over the veal.

Braised Lamb Shanks with Navy Beans

❧ SERVES 4

❧ PREPARATION TIME: 10 MINUTES

❧ COOKING TIME: 2 HOURS 15 MINUTES

2 cups dried navy beans
$1/3$ cup oil
4 lamb shanks, trimmed
$2^2/3$ tablespoons butter
2 medium garlic cloves, crushed
2 medium onions, finely chopped
$1^1/2$ tablespoons thyme
2 tablespoons concentrated tomato purée
$3^1/4$ cups canned crushed tomatoes
1 tablespoon paprika
1 dried jalapeño chili, roughly chopped
1 cup roughly chopped Italian parsley

Cover the beans with water and soak overnight.

In a large heavy-based saucepan, heat 3 tablespoons of the oil over medium heat and brown the lamb on all sides. Remove, set aside and drain the fat from the pan. Heat the butter and remaining oil in the pan and cook the garlic and onion over medium heat for 3–4 minutes, or until softened. Add the thyme, tomato purée, crushed tomato and paprika and simmer for 5 minutes. Add the lamb shanks and 2 cups hot water. Season and bring to a boil. Cover, reduce the heat and simmer gently for 30 minutes.

Drain the beans and add to the pan with the chili and 2 cups hot water. Bring to a boil, cover and simmer for another $1–1^1/2$ hours, or until the beans and the meat are tender, adding more water, $1/2$ cup at a time, if necessary. Adjust the seasoning if necessary and stir in half the parsley. Serve hot, sprinkled with parsley.

Saltimbocca

Shish Kebabs with Peppers and Herbs

❧ SERVES 4
❧ PREPARATION TIME: 20 MINUTES
❧ COOKING TIME: 5 MINUTES

2 lb 4 oz boneless leg of lamb
1 medium red bell pepper
1 medium green bell pepper
3 medium red onions
olive oil, for brushing

MARINADE
1 medium onion, thinly sliced
2 medium garlic cloves, crushed
1/4 cup lemon juice
1/3 cup olive oil
1 tablespoon chopped thyme
1 tablespoon paprika
1/2 teaspoon chii flakes
2 teaspoons ground cumin
1/2 cup chopped Italian parsley
1/3 cup chopped mint

If using wooden skewers, soak them in water for about 30 minutes to prevent them from burning during cooking.

Trim the sinew and most of the fat from the lamb and cut the meat into 1 1/4 inch cubes. Mix all the ingredients for the marinade in a large bowl. Season well, add the meat and mix well. Cover and refrigerate for 4–6 hours, or overnight.

Remove the seeds and membrane from the peppers and cut the flesh into 1 1/4 inch squares. Cut each red onion into six wedges. Remove the lamb from the marinade and reserve the liquid. Thread the meat onto the skewers, alternating with onion and pepper pieces. Broil the skewers for 5–6 minutes, brushing frequently with the marinade for the first couple of minutes. Serve immediately. These are delicious served with bread or pilaff.

Pasticcio

❧ SERVES 6
❧ PREPARATION TIME: 1 HOUR
❧ COOKING TIME: 1 HOUR 50 MINUTES

2 cups all-purpose flour
½ cup cold butter, chopped
¼ cup) superfine sugar
1 egg yolk
5½ oz bucatini or penne rigate

FILLING
2 tablespoons olive oil
1 onion, chopped
2 garlic cloves, finely chopped
1 lb 2 oz ground beef
5½ oz chicken livers
2 tomatoes, chopped
½ cup red wine
½ cup rich beef stock
1 tablespoon chopped oregano
¼ teaspoon freshly grated nutmeg
½ cup freshly grated parmesan cheese

BÉCHAMEL SAUCE
¼ cup butter
2 tablespoons all-purpose flour
1½ cups cold milk

Put the flour, butter, sugar, and egg yolk in a food processor with 1 tablespoon water. Process lightly until the mixture forms a ball, adding more water if necessary. Lightly knead the dough on a floured surface until smooth. Wrap in plastic wrap and refrigerate.

To make the filling, heat the oil in a heavy-based saucepan and cook the onion and garlic until softened and lightly golden. Increase the heat, add the beef, and cook until browned, breaking up any lumps with a fork. Add the livers, tomatoes, red wine, stock, oregano, and nutmeg, then season well. Cook the sauce over high heat until it boils, reduce to a simmer and cook, covered, for 40 minutes, then cool. Stir in the parmesan.

To make the béchamel sauce, heat the butter in a saucepan over low heat. Add the flour and stir for 1 minute, or until the mixture is golden and smooth. Remove from the heat and gradually stir in the milk. Return to the heat and stir constantly until the sauce boils and begins to thicken. Simmer for another minute. Season to taste.

Cook the pasta in a saucepan of rapidly boiling salted water until *al dente*. Drain and cool.

Preheat the oven to 325°F. Lightly grease a deep 9 inch pie dish. Divide the dough into two and roll out one piece to fit the base of the prepared dish, allowing the edges to overhang the side. Spoon about half of the meat mixture into the dish, top with the pasta, and slowly spoon the béchamel sauce over the top, allowing it to seep down and coat the pasta. Top with the remaining meat. Roll out the remaining dough and cover the pie. Trim the edges and pinch lightly to seal. Bake for 50–55 minutes, or until dark golden brown and crisp. Set aside for 15 minutes before cutting.

Veal Osso Bucco alla Milanese

🌸 SERVES 4

🌸 PREPARATION TIME: 30 MINUTES

🌸 COOKING TIME: 1 HOUR 40 MINUTES

12 pieces veal shank, about 1½ inch thick
all-purpose flour, seasoned, for dusting
¼ cup olive oil
¼ cup butter
1 medium garlic clove, finely chopped
1 medium onion, finely chopped
1 medium celery stalk, finely chopped
1 cup dry white wine
1 medium bay leaf or lemon leaf
pinch ground allspice
pinch ground cinnamon

GREMOLATA
2 teaspoons grated lemon zest
2 tablespoons finely chopped Italian
   parsley
1 medium garlic clove, finely chopped

Dust each piece of veal shank with seasoned flour. Heat the oil, butter, garlic, onion and celery in a heavy-based frying pan or saucepan that is big enough to hold the shanks in a single layer (but don't add the shanks yet). Cook for about 5 minutes over low heat until softened but not browned. Add the shanks to the pan and cook for 12–15 minutes, or until well browned all over. Arrange the shanks in the pan, standing them up in a single layer. Pour in the wine and add the bay leaf, allspice and cinnamon. Bring to a boil and cover the pan. Turn the heat down to low.

Cook at a low simmer for 15 minutes, then add ½ cup warm water. Continue cooking, covered, for 45–60 minutes (the timing will depend on the age of the veal) or until the meat is tender and you can cut it with a fork. Check the volume of liquid once or twice during cooking time and add more warm water as needed.

To make the gremolata, mix together the lemon zest, parsley and garlic.

Transfer the veal shanks to a plate and keep warm. Discard the bay leaf. Increase the heat under the pan and stir for 1–2 minutes until the sauce has thickened, scraping up any bits off the bottom of the pan as you stir. Season to taste and return the veal shanks to the sauce. Heat everything through, then stir in half the gremolata. Serve sprinkled with the remaining gremolata.

Shanghai Pork Noodles

½ teaspoon sesame oil
¼ cup soy sauce
2 tablespoons oyster sauce
9 oz pork loin fillet, cut into very thin
    strips
2 tablespoons dried shrimp
8 dried shiitake mushrooms
1 teaspoon sugar
1 cup chicken stock
10½ oz fresh Shanghai noodles
2 tablespoons peanut oil
1 garlic clove, thinly sliced
2 teaspoons grated fresh ginger
1 celery stalk, cut into matchsticks
1 leek, white part only, cut into
    matchsticks
5½ oz Chinese cabbage, shredded
¼ cup canned bamboo shoots, cut into
    matchsticks
8 scallions, thinly sliced

Combine the sesame oil and 1 tablespoon each of the soy sauce and oyster sauce in a large non-metallic bowl. Add the pork strips and toss in the marinade. Cover and marinate in the refrigerator for 30 minutes.

Meanwhile, put the dried shrimp in a bowl, cover with boiling water and soak for 20 minutes. Drain and finely chop. At the same time, put the shiitake mushrooms in a heatproof bowl, cover with boiling water and soak for 20 minutes. Drain, squeeze the mushrooms dry, discard the stems and thinly slice the caps.

To make the stir-fry sauce, combine the sugar, stock, remaining soy and oyster sauces, and 1 teaspoon salt in a small non-metallic bowl. Set aside.

Cook the noodles in a large saucepan of boiling water for 4–5 minutes, or until tender. Drain and refresh under cold water. Toss with 1 teaspoon of the peanut oil.

Heat a wok over high heat, add 1 tablespoon of the peanut oil and swirl to coat the base and side. Add the pork and stir-fry for 1–2 minutes, or until the pork is no longer pink. Transfer to a plate.

Heat the remaining peanut oil, add the garlic, ginger, celery, leek, and cabbage and stir-fry for 1 minute, or until softened. Add the bamboo shoots, scallion, shrimp and mushrooms and stir-fry for 1 minute. Add the noodles and the stir-fry sauce and toss together for 3–5 minutes, or until the noodles absorb the sauce.

Return the pork to the wok, with any juices, and toss for 1–2 minutes, or until combined and heated through. Serve immediately.

Lamb Braise with Eggplant Cream

❧ SERVES 6–8
❧ PREPARATION TIME: 30 MINUTES
❧ COOKING TIME: 1 HOUR 45 MINUTES

2 tablespoons olive oil
2 lb 4 oz lamb, cut into ¾ inch cubes
1 large onion, chopped
1 bay leaf
small pinch ground cloves
2 garlic cloves, crushed
2 tablespoons concentrated tomato purée
1²/₃ cups canned chopped tomatoes
¾ cup chopped Italian parsley, plus extra,
    to garnish
3 cups beef stock
4½ oz vine-ripened tomatoes, chopped

EGGPLANT CREAM
2 lb 4 oz eggplants
¼ cup butter
2½ tablespoons all-purpose flour
1¼ cups whipping cream
²/₃ cup grated kasseri cheese (see Note)
large pinch freshly grated nutmeg

Heat the oil in a large, deep saucepan over high heat and cook the lamb in three batches for 4–5 minutes, or until well browned. Remove the lamb from the pan with a slotted spoon and set aside.

Add the onion to the pan, cook for 5 minutes, or until golden, then add the bay leaf, cloves, garlic, tomato purée, tomatoes, parsley, stock, and lamb and stir well. Bring to a boil, then reduce the heat to low, cover, and simmer, stirring occasionally for 1½ hours, or until the lamb is tender and the sauce is thick. Season.

Meanwhile, to make the eggplant cream, preheat the oven to 400°F. Pierce the eggplants a few times with a fork and, using a long-handled fork, roast them over an open flame (either a gas stovetop or a barbecue) for about 5 minutes, turning occasionally, until blackened and blistered all over. This will give them a good smoky flavor. Place the eggplants on a baking sheet and bake for about 30 minutes, or until the eggplants are shrivelled and the flesh is very soft. Transfer to a colander and leave to cool.

When cool, peel the eggplants, ensuring all the skin is removed and discarded. Chop the flesh and set aside. Melt the butter in a saucepan over medium heat and add the flour. Stir for 2 minutes, or until it has a toasty aroma and darkens slightly. Gradually pour in the cream, whisking until smooth, then stir in the eggplant. Add the cheese and nutmeg and stir until the cheese has melted. Season.

Spread the eggplant cream on a serving plate, place the lamb in the center and sprinkle with the chopped tomato and parsley. Serve immediately.

NOTE: Kasseri cheese, available at specialist delicatessens, is a sheep or goat's milk cheese, often used on top of lamb stews.

Roast Sirloin with Mustard Sauce

☙ SERVES 6

☙ PREPARATION TIME: 15 MINUTES

☙ COOKING TIME: 1 HOUR 15 MINUTES

3 lb 5 oz beef sirloin
1/3 cup wholegrain mustard
1 tablespoon dijon mustard
1 teaspoon honey
1 medium garlic clove, crushed
1 tablespoon oil

MUSTARD SAUCE
1 cup white wine
1 tablespoon dijon mustard
1/4 cup wholegrain mustard
2 tablespoons honey
3/4 cup cubed chilled butter

Preheat the oven to 425°F. Cut most of the fat from the piece of beef sirloin, leaving a thin layer. Mix together the mustards and add the honey and garlic. Spread over the sirloin in a thick layer. Place the oil in an ovenproof dish and heat it in the oven for 2 minutes. Place the meat in the hot dish and roast for 15 minutes. Reduce the oven to 400°F and cook for 45–50 minutes for medium-rare, or until cooked to your liking.

To make the sauce, pour the wine into a saucepan and cook over high heat for 5 minutes, or until reduced by half. Add the mustards and honey. Reduce the heat and whisk in the butter. Remove from the heat and season. Serve thin slices of the meat with the sauce and roast vegetables.

Lamb Crown Roast with Sage Stuffing

☙ SERVES 4–6

☙ PREPARATION TIME: 30 MINUTES

☙ COOKING TIME: 50 MINUTES

1 crown roast of lamb (12 cutlets)
1 1/3 tablespoons butter
2 medium onions, chopped
1 medium granny smith apple, peeled and
    chopped
2 cups fresh breadcrumbs
2 tablespoons chopped sage
1 tablespoon chopped Italian parsley
1/4 cup unsweetened apple juice
2 eggs, separated

Preheat the oven to 425°F. Trim the meat of excess fat and sinew.

Melt the butter in a saucepan. Add the onion and apple and cook over medium heat until soft. Remove from the heat and stir into the combined breadcrumbs, sage and parsley. Whisk the apple juice and egg yolks together, then stir into the breadcrumb mixture. Beat the egg whites using electric beaters until soft peaks form. Fold into the stuffing mixture.

Place the roast on a sheet of greased foil in an ovenproof dish. Wrap some foil around the tops of the bones to prevent burning. Spoon the stuffing into the cavity. Roast for 45 minutes for medium, or until cooked to your liking. Leave for 10 minutes before cutting between the cutlets.

Roast Sirloin with Mustard Sauce

Tagliatelle with Veal, Wine and Cream

❀ SERVES 4
❀ PREPARATION TIME: 15 MINUTES
❀ COOKING TIME: 20 MINUTES

1 lb 2 oz thin strips veal scaloppine or
    escalopes
all-purpose flour, seasoned
¼ cup butter
1 medium onion, sliced
½ cup dry white wine
¼ cup beef stock or chicken stock
⅔ cup whipping cream
1 lb 5 oz fresh plain or spinach
    tagliatelle (or a mixture of both)
1 tablespoon freshly grated parmesan
    cheese, plus extra, to serve, optional
Italian parsley, to garnish

Coat the veal strips with the seasoned flour. Melt the butter in a frying pan. Add the veal strips and fry quickly until browned. Remove with a slotted spoon and set aside.

Add the onion to the pan and stir until soft and golden. Pour in the wine and cook rapidly to reduce the liquid. Add the stock and cream and season to taste. Reduce the sauce again, and add the veal towards the end.

Meanwhile, cook the tagliatelle in a large saucepan of rapidly boiling salted water until *al dente*. Drain and transfer to a warm serving dish.

Stir the parmesan through the sauce. Pour the sauce over the pasta. Serve with extra parmesan, if desired, and garnish with parsley.

Slow~Roasted Lamb with Cumin and Paprika

❀ SERVES 6
❀ PREPARATION TIME: 15 MINUTES
❀ COOKING TIME: 3 HOURS 30 MINUTES

5 lb leg of lamb
⅓ cup softened butter
3 medium garlic cloves, crushed
2 teaspoons ground cumin
3 teaspoons ground coriander
1 teaspoon paprika
1 tablespoon ground cumin, extra,
    for dipping

Preheat the oven to 425°F. With a small sharp knife, cut small deep slits in the top and sides of the lamb.

Mix the butter, garlic, spices and ¼ teaspoon salt in a bowl until a smooth paste forms.

With the back of a spoon, rub the paste all over the lamb, then use your fingers to spread the paste and make sure all the lamb is covered.

Put the lamb, bone side down, in a deep roasting pan and place on the top shelf of the oven. Bake for 10 minutes, then baste and return to the oven. Reduce the temperature to 325°F. Bake for 3 hours 20 minutes, basting every 20–30 minutes. Basting makes the lamb tender and flavorsome. Carve the lamb into chunky slices. Mix the cumin with 1½ teaspoons salt and serve on the side for dipping.

Tagliatelle with Veal, Wine and Cream

Rabbit Casserole with Mustard Sauce

* SERVES 4–6
* PREPARATION TIME: 30 MINUTES
* COOKING TIME: 2 HOURS

2 x 1 lb 12 oz rabbits
2 tablespoons olive oil
2 onions, sliced
4 bacon slices, cut into 1¼ inch pieces
2 tablespoons all-purpose flour
1½ cups chicken stock
½ cup dry white wine
1 teaspoon thyme leaves
½ cup whipping cream
2 tablespoons dijon mustard
thyme sprigs, to garnish

Preheat the oven to 350°F. Wash the rabbits under cold water and pat dry with paper towels. Cut along both sides of each backbone with kitchen scissors and discard. Cut each rabbit into eight even-sized pieces, remove any fat, and pat dry again.

Heat half the oil in a 10-cup capacity flameproof casserole dish. Brown the rabbit in batches, adding more oil when necessary, then remove from the dish.

Add the onion and bacon to the casserole dish and cook, stirring, for 5 minutes, or until lightly browned. Sprinkle the flour into the dish and mix. Stir with a wooden spoon to scrape tany residue from the base. Add the stock and wine, and stir until the sauce comes to a boil. Return the rabbit to the casserole dish and add the thyme leaves.

Cover and bake for 1¼–1½ hours, or until the rabbit is tender and the sauce has thickened. Stir in the combined cream and mustard. Garnish with thyme sprigs. Serve with steamed vegetables.

Beef Pie

☙ SERVES 6
☙ PREPARATION TIME: 35 MINUTES
☙ COOKING TIME: 2 HOURS 45 MINUTES

FILLING
2 tablespoons olive oil
2 lb 4 oz trimmed chuck steak, cubed
1 large onion, chopped
1 large carrot, finely chopped
2 garlic cloves, crushed
2 tablespoons all-purpose flour
1 cup beef stock
2 teaspoons thyme
1 tablespoon worcestershire sauce

PASTRY
2 cups all-purpose flour
2/3 cup chilled butter, cubed
1 egg yolk
2–3 tablespoons iced water

1 egg yolk, to glaze
1 tablespoon milk, to glaze

Lightly grease a 9 inch pie dish. To make the filling, heat half of the oil in a large frying pan and brown the meat in batches. Remove from the pan. Heat the remaining oil, add the onion, carrot, and garlic and brown over medium heat. Return the meat to the pan and stir in the flour. Cook for 1 minute, then remove from the heat and slowly stir in the stock, mixing the flour in well. Add the thyme and worcestershire sauce and bring to a boil. Season to taste.

Reduce the heat to very low, cover and simmer for 1 1/2–2 hours, or until the meat is tender. During the last 15 minutes of cooking, remove the lid and allow the liquid to reduce so that the sauce is very thick and suitable for filling a pie. Allow to cool completely.

To make the pastry, sift the flour into a large bowl. Using your fingertips, rub in the butter until it resembles fine breadcrumbs. Add the egg yolk and 2 tablespoons of the water and mix with a flat-bladed knife, using a cutting action, until the mixture comes together in beads. Add more water if the dough is too dry. Turn out onto a lightly floured work surface and gather together to form a smooth dough. Wrap in plastic wrap and refrigerate for 30 minutes.

Preheat the oven to 400°F. Divide the pastry in half and roll out one piece between two sheets of parchment paper until large enough to line the pie dish. Line the dish with the pastry, fill with the cold filling, and brush the pastry edges with water. Roll out the remaining pastry to cover the dish. Lay the pastry over the pie and gently press or pinch to seal the edges. Trim any excess pastry. Re-roll the scraps to make decorative shapes and press onto the pie.

Cut a few steam holes in the top of the pastry. Beat together the egg yolk and milk and brush over the top of the pie. Bake for 20–30 minutes, or until the pastry is golden and the filling is hot.

Classic Lasagne

* SERVES 8
* PREPARATION TIME: 40 MINUTES
* COOKING TIME: 1 HOUR 40 MINUTES

2 tablespoons olive oil
1 1/2 tablespoons butter
1 large onion, finely chopped
1 carrot, finely chopped
1 celery stalk, finely chopped
1 lb 2 oz ground beef
5 1/2 oz chicken livers, finely chopped
1 cup puréed tomatoes
1 cup red wine
2 tablespoons chopped Italian parsley
13 oz fresh lasagne sheets
1 cup freshly grated parmesan cheese

BÉCHAMEL SAUCE
1/4 cup butter
1/3 cup) all-purpose flour
2 1/4 cups milk
1/2 teaspoon freshly grated nutmeg

Heat the oil and butter in a heavy-based frying pan and cook the onion, carrot, and celery over medium heat until softened, stirring constantly. Increase the heat, add the beef and brown well, breaking up any lumps with a fork. Add the chicken livers and cook until they change color. Add the tomato purée, wine, parsley, and season to taste. Bring to a boil, reduce the heat, and simmer for 45 minutes, then set aside.

To make the béchamel sauce, melt the butter in a saucepan over low heat. Add the flour and stir for 1 minute. Remove from the heat and gradually stir in the milk. Return to the heat and stir constantly until the sauce boils and begins to thicken. Simmer for another minute. Add the nutmeg and season to taste. Place a piece of plastic wrap on the surface of the sauce to prevent a skin forming, and set aside.

Cut the lasagne sheets to fit into a deep, rectangular ovenproof dish.

To assemble, preheat the oven to 350°F. Grease the ovenproof dish. Spread a thin layer of the meat sauce over the base and follow with a thin layer of béchamel. If the béchamel has cooled and become too thick, warm it gently to make spreading easier. Lay the lasagne sheets on top, gently pressing to push out any air. Continue the layers, finishing with the béchamel. Sprinkle with the parmesan and bake for about 40 minutes, or until golden brown. Cool for 15 minutes before cutting.

NOTE: Instant lasagne can be used instead of fresh. Follow the manufacturer's instructions. If you prefer, you can leave out the chicken livers and increase the amount of ground meat.

Roast Beef with Yorkshire Puddings

❀ SERVES 6–8
❀ PREPARATION TIME: 15 MINUTES
❀ COOKING TIME: 1 HOUR 40 MINUTES

4 lb 8 oz piece roasting beef
    (scotch fillet, rump or sirloin)
2 medium garlic cloves, crushed

YORKSHIRE PUDDINGS
3/4 cup all-purpose flour
1/2 cup whole milk
2 eggs

RED WINE GRAVY
2 tablespoons all-purpose flour
1/3 cup red wine
2 1/2 cups beef stock

Preheat the oven to 475°F. Rub the piece of beef with the crushed garlic and some freshly cracked black pepper and drizzle with oil. Bake on a rack in an ovenproof dish for 20 minutes.

To make the Yorkshire puddings, sift the flour and 1/2 teaspoon salt into a large bowl, then make a well in the center and whisk in the milk. In a separate bowl, whisk the eggs together until fluffy, then add to the batter and mix well. Add 1/2 cup water and whisk until large bubbles form on the surface. Cover the bowl with plastic wrap and refrigerate for 1 hour.

Reduce the oven to 350°F and continue to roast the meat for 1 hour for rare, or longer for well-done. Cover loosely with foil and leave in a warm place while making the Yorkshire puddings.

Increase the oven to 425°F. Pour off all the pan juices into a cup and spoon 1/2 teaspoon of the juices into 12 1/3-cup muffin pans. (Reserve the remaining juice for the gravy.) Heat the muffin pans in the oven until the fat is almost smoking. Whisk the batter again until bubbles form on the surface. Pour into each muffin pan to three-quarters full. Bake for 20 minutes, or until puffed and lightly golden. Make the gravy while the Yorkshire puddings are baking.

To make the gravy, heat 2 tablespoons of the reserved pan juices in the ovenproof dish on the stovetop over low heat. Add the flour and stir well, scraping the dish to incorporate all the sediment. Cook over medium heat for 1–2 minutes, stirring constantly, until the flour is well browned. Remove from the heat and gradually stir in the wine and stock. Return to the heat, stirring constantly, until the gravy boils and thickens. Simmer for 3 minutes, then season, to taste, with salt and freshly ground black pepper. Strain, if desired.

Serve the beef with the hot Yorkshire puddings and red wine gravy.

Baked Cannelloni Milanese

⁂ SERVES 4
⁂ PREPARATION TIME: 40 MINUTES
⁂ COOKING TIME: 1 HOUR 35 MINUTES

1 lb 2 oz ground pork and veal
1/2 cup dry breadcrumbs
2 eggs, beaten
1 teaspoon dried oregano
1 cup freshly grated parmesan cheese
12–15 instant cannelloni tubes
1 1/2 cups fresh ricotta cheese
1/2 cup freshly grated cheddar cheese

TOMATO SAUCE
1 3/4 cups canned puréed tomatoes
1 3/4 cups canned crushed tomatoes
2 garlic cloves, crushed
3 tablespoons chopped basil

Preheat the oven to 350°F. Lightly grease a deep rectangular casserole dish.

In a bowl, combine the pork and veal mince, breadcrumbs, egg, oregano, and half the parmesan, and season to taste. Use a teaspoon to stuff the cannelloni tubes with the mixture. Set aside.

To make the tomato sauce, bring the tomato purée, tomatoes, and garlic to a boil in a saucepan. Reduce the heat and simmer for 15 minutes. Add the basil and pepper, to taste, and stir well.

Spoon half the tomato sauce over the base of the prepared dish. Arrange the stuffed cannelloni tubes on top. Cover with the remaining sauce. Spread with ricotta cheese. Sprinkle with the combined remaining parmesan and cheddar cheese. Bake, covered with foil, for 1 hour. Uncover and bake for another 15 minutes, or until golden. Cut into squares to serve.

Beef Provençale

❀ SERVES 6
❀ PREPARATION TIME: 20 MINUTES
❀ COOKING TIME: 2 HOURS 25 MINUTES

3 lb 5 oz chuck steak, cut into 1½ inch
    pieces
2 tablespoons olive oil
1 small onion, sliced
1½ cups red wine
2 tablespoons chopped Italian parsley
1 tablespoon chopped rosemary
1 tablespoon chopped thyme
9 oz speck, rind removed, cut into
    ½ x ¾ inch pieces
1⅔ cups canned crushed tomatoes
1 cup beef stock
30 baby carrots
⅓ cup pitted medium niçoise olives

In a bowl, combine the cubed beef with 1 tablespoon of the oil, the onion, 1 cup of the wine and half the herbs. Cover with plastic wrap and marinate in the refrigerator overnight. Drain the beef, reserving the marinade. Heat the remaining oil in a large heavy-based saucepan and brown the beef and onion in batches. Remove from the pan.

Add the speck to the saucepan and cook for 3–5 minutes, or until crisp. Return the beef to the pan with the remaining wine and marinade and cook, scraping the residue from the base of the pan for 2 minutes, or until the wine has slightly reduced. Add the tomato and stock and bring to a boil. Reduce the heat and add the remaining herbs. Season well, cover and simmer for 1½ hours.

Add the carrots and olives to the saucepan and cook, uncovered, for another 30 minutes, or until the meat and the carrots are tender. Before serving, check the seasoning and adjust if necessary.

vegetables

Lemon and Herb Risotto with Fried Mushrooms

- SERVES 4–6
- PREPARATION TIME: 30 MINUTES
- COOKING TIME: 50 MINUTES

4 cups chicken or vegetable stock
pinch saffron threads
2 tablespoons olive oil
2 leeks, thinly sliced
2 medium garlic cloves, crushed
2 cups risotto rice
2–3 teaspoons finely grated lemon zest
2 tablespoons lemon juice
2 tablespoons chopped Italian parsley
2 tablespoons snipped chives
2 tablespoons chopped oregano
$3/4$ cup freshly grated parmesan cheese
$1/2$ cup mascarpone cheese
2 tablespoons butter
1 tablespoon olive oil
$2^1/4$ cups thickly sliced white mushrooms
1 tablespoon balsamic vinegar

Pour the stock into a saucepan and add the saffron threads. Bring to a boil, then reduce the heat, cover and keep at a low simmer.

Heat the olive oil in a large saucepan over medium heat. Add the leek, cook for 5 minutes, then add the garlic and cook for a further 5 minutes, or until golden. Add the rice and stir until well coated. Add half the lemon zest and half the juice, then add $1/2$ cup of the hot stock. Stir constantly over medium heat until all the liquid has been absorbed. Continue adding more liquid, $1/2$ cup at a time, until all the liquid is absorbed and the rice is tender and creamy. (You may not need to use all the stock, or you may need a little extra — every risotto will be slightly different.)

Remove the pan from the heat. Stir in the herbs, parmesan, mascarpone and the remaining lemon zest and lemon juice. Cover and keep warm.

To cook the mushrooms, melt the butter and olive oil in a large frying pan, add the mushroom slices and vinegar and cook, stirring, over high heat for 5–7 minutes, or until the mushrooms are tender and all the liquid has been absorbed.

Serve the risotto in large bowls topped with the mushrooms.

Cranberry Bean Moussaka

❧ SERVES 6
❧ PREPARATION TIME: 45 MINUTES
❧ COOKING TIME: 2 HOURS 30 MINUTES

1 1/4 cups dried cranberry beans
2 large eggplants
1/3 cup olive oil
1 garlic clove, crushed
1 onion, chopped
1 1/2 cups sliced white mushrooms
3 1/2 cups canned chopped tomatoes
1 cup red wine
1 tablespoon concentrated tomato purée
1 tablespoon chopped oregano

TOPPING
1 cup plain yogurt
4 eggs, lightly beaten
2 cups milk
1/4 teaspoon paprika
1/2 cup freshly grated parmesan cheese
1/2 cup fresh breadcrumbs

Soak the cranberry beans in cold water overnight. Rinse and drain well.

Put the cranberry beans in a large heavy-based saucepan, cover with water and bring to a boil. Reduce the heat and simmer for 1 1/2 hours, or until tender. Drain the beans.

Meanwhile, slice the eggplant, sprinkle with salt and set aside for 30 minutes. Rinse and pat dry. Brush the eggplant slices with a little of the oil and cook under a preheated broiler for 3 minutes each side, or until golden. Drain on paper towels.

Preheat the oven to 400°F. Heat the remaining oil in a large heavy-based saucepan. Add the garlic and onion and cook over medium heat for 3 minutes, or until the onion is golden. Add the mushrooms and cook for 3 minutes, or until browned. Stir in the tomatoes, wine, tomato purée and oregano. Bring to a boil, reduce the heat and simmer for 40 minutes, or until the sauce has thickened.

To assemble the moussaka, spoon the cranberry beans into a large, ovenproof dish and top with the tomato sauce and eggplant slices.

To make the topping, whisk together the yogurt, eggs, milk and paprika. Pour over the eggplant and set aside for 10 minutes. Combine the parmesan cheese and breadcrumbs and sprinkle over the moussaka. Bake for 45–60 minutes, or until the moussaka is heated through and the top is golden.

Tofu, Peanut and Noodle Stir-Fry

❀ SERVES 4
❀ PREPARATION TIME: 15 MINUTES
❀ COOKING TIME: 5 MINUTES

1 medium red bell pepper
1 1/3 cups firm tofu
1 medium onion
2 cups broccoli
2 medium garlic cloves, crushed
1 teaspoon grated fresh ginger
1/3 cup kecap manis
1/3 cup peanut butter
2 tablespoons peanut or vegetable oil
1 lb 2 oz hokkien (egg) noodles

Cut the pepper in half, remove the seeds and membrane and chop. Cut the tofu into 5/8 inch cubes. Chop the onion and cut the broccoli into small florets. Combine the tofu with the garlic, ginger and half the kecap manis in a small bowl. Put the peanut butter, 1/2 cup water and remaining kecap manis in another bowl and mix.

Heat a wok over high heat, add the oil and swirl to coat the base and side. Drain the tofu and reserve the marinade. Cook the tofu in two batches in the hot oil until well browned. Remove from the wok.

Put the noodles in a large heatproof bowl. Cover with boiling water and leave for 1 minute. Drain and gently separate the noodles. Add the vegetables to the wok (add a little more oil if necessary) and stir-fry until just tender. Add the tofu, reserved marinade and noodles to the wok. Add the peanut butter mixture and toss until heated through.

Linguine with Roasted Vegetable Sauce

❀ SERVES 4
❀ PREPARATION TIME: 30 MINUTES
❀ COOKING TIME: 50 MINUTES

4 large red bell peppers
1 lb 2 oz firm ripe medium tomatoes
3 large red onions
1 bulb garlic
1/2 cup balsamic vinegar
1/4 cup olive oil
2 teaspoons sea salt
2 teaspoons freshly ground black pepper
1 lb 2 oz linguine
1 cup shaved parmesan cheese
1/2 cup medium black olives

Preheat the oven to 350°F. Cut the peppers in half and remove the seeds and membrane. Cut the tomatoes and onions in half and separate and peel the garlic cloves.

Arrange the vegetables in a large ovenproof dish in a single layer. Pour the vinegar and oil over them and sprinkle with the sea salt and pepper. Bake for 50 minutes. Allow to cool for 5 minutes before puréeing in a food processor for 3 minutes, or until the mixture is smooth. Season with more salt and pepper, if necessary.

When the vegetables are almost cooked, cook the linguine in a large saucepan of rapidly boiling salted water until *al dente*. Drain. Serve the roasted vegetable sauce over the linguine with the parmesan cheese, olives and some extra black pepper.

Tofu, Peanut and Noodle Stir-Fry

Spicy Chickpea and Vegetable Casserole

※ SERVES 4
※ PREPARATION TIME: 25 MINUTES
※ COOKING TIME: 1 HOUR 30 MINUTES

1½ cups dried chickpeas (see Note)
1 large onion
2 cups winter squash
1¼ cups green beans
7 oz pattypan squash
2 tablespoons oil
1 medium garlic clove, crushed
3 teaspoons ground cumin
½ teaspoon chili powder
½ teaspoon ground allspice
1¾ cups canned crushed tomatoes
1½ cups vegetable stock
2 tablespoons concentrated tomato purée
1 teaspoon dried oregano

Put the chickpeas in a large bowl. Cover with cold water and soak overnight. Drain.

Chop the onion. Cut the winter squash into large cubes. Top and tail the beans. Cut the pattypan squash into quarters.

Heat the oil in a large saucepan. Add the onion and garlic and stir-fry for 2 minutes, or until tender. Add the cumin, chili powder and allspice. Stir-fry for 1 minute. Add the chickpeas, tomatoes and vegetable stock to the pan. Bring to a boil, then reduce the heat and simmer, covered, for 1 hour, stirring occasionally.

Add the winter squash, beans, button squash, concentrated tomato purée and oregano. Stir to combine. Simmer, covered, for another 15 minutes. Remove the lid from the pan and simmer, uncovered, for another 10 minutes to reduce and slightly thicken the sauce.

NOTE: A quick way to soak chickpeas is to place them in a large saucepan and cover with cold water. Bring to a boil, then remove from the heat and soak for 2 hours. If you are in a hurry, substitute canned chickpeas. Drain and rinse thoroughly before use.

Vegetable Lasagne

🌿 SERVES 6

🌿 PREPARATION TIME: 40 MINUTES

🌿 COOKING TIME: 1 HOUR 15 MINUTES

3 large red peppers
2 large eggplants
2 tablespoons olive oil
1 large onion, chopped
3 garlic cloves, crushed
1 teaspoon dried mixed herbs
1 teaspoon dried oregano
5½ cups mushrooms, sliced
1¾ cups canned crushed tomatoes
440 g (15½ oz) canned red kidney beans,
    drained
1 tablespoon sweet chili sauce
9 oz package instant lasagne
1 lb 2 oz spinach, chopped
¾ cup basil leaves
½ cup sliced sun-dried tomatoes
¼ cup grated parmesan cheese
¼ cup grated cheddar cheese

CHEESE SAUCE
¼ cup butter
¼ cup all-purpose flour
2 cups milk
2½ cups ricotta cheese

Preheat the oven to 350°F. Brush an 11¼ x 14 inch ovenproof dish with oil.

Cut the pepper in half, remove the seeds and membrane and cut into large flattish pieces. Cook, skin side up, under a hot broiler for 8 minutes, or until the skin is black and blistered. Cover with a damp dish towel and when cool, peel away the skin and cut the flesh into long thin strips. Set aside.

Slice the eggplant into ½ inch rounds and put in a large saucepan of boiling water. Cook for 1 minute, or until just tender. Drain, pat dry with paper towels and set aside.

Heat the oil in a large heavy-based frying pan and add the onion, garlic, and herbs. Cook over medium heat for 5 minutes, or until the onion is soft. Add the mushrooms and cook for 1 minute. Add the crushed tomatoes, red kidney beans, chili sauce and season to taste. Bring to a boil, reduce the heat and simmer for 15 minutes, or until the sauce thickens. Remove from the heat and set aside.

To make the cheese sauce, heat the butter in a saucepan and stir in the flour over medium heat for 1 minute, or until smooth. Remove from the heat and gradually stir in the milk. Return to the heat and stir constantly until the sauce boils and begins to thicken. Simmer for another minute. Add the ricotta and stir until smooth.

Dip the lasagne sheets, if necessary, in hot water to soften slightly and arrange four sheets on the base of the dish. Build up layers on top of the pasta, using half of the eggplant, spinach, basil, grilled pepper strips, mushroom sauce and then the sun-dried tomatoes. Top with a layer of pasta and press gently. Repeat the layers, finishing with a layer of lasagne. Top with cheese sauce and sprinkle with the combined parmesan and cheddar cheeses. Bake for 45 minutes, or until the pasta is soft.

Pea, Egg and Ricotta Curry

❋ SERVES 4
❋ PREPARATION TIME: 15 MINUTES
❋ COOKING TIME: 30 MINUTES

4 hard-boiled eggs
$1/2$ teaspoon ground turmeric
2 small onions
$4\frac{1}{2}$ oz baked ricotta cheese (see Note)
3 tablespoons ghee or oil
1 medium bay leaf
1 teaspoon finely chopped garlic
$1\frac{1}{2}$ teaspoons ground coriander
$1\frac{1}{2}$ teaspoons garam masala
$1/2$ teaspoon chili powder, optional
$1/2$ cup canned chopped tomatoes
1 tablespoon concentrated tomato purée
1 tablespoon plain yogurt
$1/2$ cup frozen peas
2 tablespoons finely chopped cilantro
  leaves

Peel the eggs and coat them with the turmeric. Finely chop the onion and cut the ricotta into $1/2$ inch cubes.

Melt the ghee in a large saucepan and cook the eggs over moderate heat for 2 minutes until they are light brown, stirring constantly. Set aside.

Add the bay leaf, onion and garlic to the pan and cook over moderately high heat, stirring frequently, until the mixture is well reduced and pale gold. Lower the heat if the mixture is browning too quickly. Add the ground coriander, garam masala and chili powder, if using, and cook until fragrant.

Add the chopped tomato, concentrated tomato purée and $1/2$ cup water. Cover and simmer for 5 minutes. Return the eggs to the pan with the ricotta, yogurt, peas and $1/4$ teaspoon salt and cook for 5 minutes. Remove the bay leaf, sprinkle with the cilantro and serve immediately.

NOTE: Baked ricotta cheese is available from delicatessens and some supermarkets, but it is easy to prepare your own. Preheat the oven to 325°F. Slice the required amount of fresh ricotta (not cottage cheese or blended ricotta) into $1\frac{1}{4}$ inch thick slices. Place the ricotta on a lightly greased baking sheet and bake for 25 minutes.

Spanokopita

‖ SERVES 4–6
‖ PREPARATION TIME: 25 MINUTES
‖ COOKING TIME: 1 HOUR

3 lb 5 oz Swiss chard
¼ cup olive oil
1 white onion, finely chopped
10 scallions, finely chopped
1½ tablespoons chopped dill
1⅓ cups Greek feta cheese, crumbled
½ cup cottage cheese
⅓ cup finely grated kefalotyri cheese
    (see Note)
¼ teaspoon freshly grated nutmeg
4 eggs, lightly beaten
10 sheets filo pastry
⅓ cup butter, melted, to brush

Rinse and drain the Swiss chard thoroughly. Discard the stems and shred the leaves. Finely chop the onion.

Heat the olive oil in a large frying pan, add the onion and cook, stirring, over medium heat for 5 minutes, or until softened. Add the scallion and Swiss chard and cook, covered, over medium heat for 5 minutes. Add the dill and cook, uncovered, for 3–4 minutes, or until most of the liquid has evaporated. Remove from the heat and cool to room temperature.

Preheat the oven to 350°F and lightly grease a large ovenproof dish with a 10-cup capacity. Put the feta, cottage cheese and kefalotyri in a large bowl. Stir in the Swiss chard mixture and add the nutmeg. Gradually add the eggs and combine well. Season to taste.

Line the base and sides of the dish with a sheet of filo pastry – keep the rest covered with a damp dish towel to prevent them from drying out. Brush with some of the melted butter and cover with another sheet of pastry. Butter the sheet and repeat in this way, using five sheets of pastry. Spoon the filling into the dish and level the surface. Fold the exposed pastry up and over to cover the top of the filling. Cover with a sheet of pastry, brush with the butter and continue until all the remaining sheets are used. Roughly trim the pastry with kitchen scissors then tuck the excess inside the wall of the dish.

Brush the top with the butter. Using a sharp knife, score the surface into squares. Sprinkle a few drops of cold water on top to prevent the pastry from curling. Bake for 45 minutes, or until puffed and golden. Rest at room temperature for 10 minutes before serving.

NOTE: Kefalotyri is a Greek cheese made from 100% pasteurized sheep's milk. It is a hard pale golden-yellow cheese with a tangy flavor and sharp aroma. It is usually grated, like parmesan or pecorino. You can use pecorino if kefalotyri is unavailable.

Lentil Bhuja Casserole

※ SERVES 4–6
※ PREPARATION TIME: 40 MINUTES
※ COOKING TIME: 1 HOUR 10 MINUTES

2 cups green lentils
1 large onion
1 large potato
1 teaspoon ground cumin
1 teaspoon ground coriander
1 teaspoon ground turmeric
³⁄₄ cup all-purpose flour
vegetable oil, for pan-frying
2 tablespoons vegetable oil, extra
2 garlic cloves, crushed
1 tablespoon grated fresh ginger
1 cup puréed tomatoes
2 cups vegetable stock
1 cup whipping cream
7 oz green beans, topped and tailed
2 carrots, sliced
pita bread, to serve

Cover the lentils with cold water and soak overnight. Drain well.

Grate the onion and potato and drain the excess liquid. Combine the lentils, onion, potato, cumin, ground coriander, turmeric and flour in a bowl, and mix well. Roll the mixture into walnut-sized balls and place them on a foil-lined baking sheet. Cover and refrigerate for 30 minutes.

Heat the oil, about ³⁄₄ inch deep, in a frying pan. Add the lentil balls in small batches and fry over high heat for 5 minutes, or until golden brown. Drain on paper towels.

Heat the extra oil in a large saucepan. Add the garlic and ginger and cook, stirring, over medium heat for 1 minute. Stir in the puréed tomatoes, vegetable stock and cream. Bring to a boil, reduce the heat and simmer, uncovered, for 10 minutes. Add the lentil balls, beans and carrot, cover and simmer for 35 minutes, stirring occasionally. Serve with pita bread.

NOTE: Make sure your hands are dry when shaping the lentil mixture into balls. The lentil balls can be made a day ahead and stored in an airtight container in the refrigerator.

Filo Risotto Pie

⚘ SERVES 8
⚘ PREPARATION TIME: 45 MINUTES
⚘ COOKING TIME: 1 HOUR 45 MINUTES

2 large red bell peppers
10 sheets filo pastry
¼ cup olive oil
2½ cups spinach, blanched
1¾ cups sliced feta cheese
1 tablespoon sesame seeds

RISOTTO

1 cup white wine
4 cups vegetable stock
2 tablespoons oil
1 medium garlic clove, crushed
1 leek, white part only, sliced
1 fennel bulb, thinly sliced
2 cups risotto rice
⅔ cup freshly grated parmesan cheese

Cut the red peppers in half. Remove the seeds and membrane and then cut into large, flattish pieces. Broil until the skin blackens and blisters. Place on a cutting board, cover with a dish towel and allow to cool. Peel the peppers and cut the flesh into smaller pieces.

To make the risotto, put the wine and stock into a large saucepan. Bring to a boil and reduce the heat.

Heat the oil and garlic in a large heavy-based saucepan. Add the leek and fennel, cook over medium heat for 5 minutes, or until lightly browned. Add the rice and stir for 3 minutes, or until the rice is translucent.

Add 1 cup of the stock mixture to the rice and stir constantly until the liquid is absorbed. Continue adding liquid, ½ cup at a time, stirring constantly until all the stock mixture has been used and the rice is tender. (This will take about 40 minutes.) Make sure the liquid stays hot as the risotto will become gluggy if it isn't. Remove from the heat, stir in the parmesan and season. Set aside until cooled slightly.

Brush each sheet of filo with olive oil and fold in half lengthways. Arrange like overlapping spokes on a wheel, in a 9 inch spring-form pan, with one side of the pastry hanging over the side of pan.

Preheat the oven to 350°F. Spoon half the risotto mixture over the pastry and top with half the red pepper, half the spinach and half the feta. Repeat with the remaining risotto, pepper, spinach and feta.

Fold the pastry over the filling, brush lightly with oil and sprinkle with sesame seeds. Bake for 50 minutes, or until the pastry is crisp and golden and the pie is heated through.

Vegetable Donburi

※ SERVES 4
※ PREPARATION TIME: 20 MINUTES
※ COOKING TIME: 35 MINUTES

3 1/2 oz green beans
2 slender eggplants
5 scallions
2 cups Japanese short-grain rice
1/4 oz dried whole shiitake mushrooms
2 tablespoons vegetable oil
1 onion, sliced
3 1/2 fl oz shoyu (Japanese soy sauce)
    (see Note)
3 1/2 fl oz mirin
1/4 cup sugar
4 eggs, lightly beaten

Trim the green beans and cut them into 1 1/2 inch lengths. Slice the eggplants diagonally and cut the scallions into 3/4 inch lengths.

Wash the rice and put in a saucepan with 2 1/2 cups water. Bring to a boil then reduce the heat and simmer, covered, for 15 minutes. Remove from the ehat and leave, covered, for 10 minutes.

Meanwhile, soak the mushrooms in 1 2/3 cups boiling water for 15 minutes. Drain and reserve the soaking liquid. Remove the stems and cut the caps in half.

Heat the oil in a deep frying pan. Cook the onion over medium heat for 4 minutes, or until softened but not browned. Add the eggplant and cook for 3–4 minutes, or until softened. Add the beans, mushrooms and scallion and cook for about 3 minutes, or until almost cooked. Combine the shoyu, mushroom soaking liquid, mirin, and sugar, and stir through the vegetables. Simmer for 4 minutes.

Pour the egg over the vegetables, cover and simmer for 1 minute, or until partly cooked. Serve the rice in bowls, spoon on the vegetable mixture and pour on the cooking sauce.

NOTE: Shoyu (Japanese soy sauce) is available from Asian speciality food stores.

Giant Shell Pasta with Ricotta and Arugula

⚜ SERVES 6

⚜ PREPARATION TIME: 50 MINUTES

⚜ COOKING TIME: 1 HOUR

40 giant shell pasta
2⅓ cups bottled pasta sauce
2 tablespoons oregano, chopped
2 tablespoons basil

FILLING

2 cups ricotta cheese
1 cup grated parmesan cheese
3 cups finely shredded arugula
1 egg, lightly beaten
¾ cup finely chopped marinated
   artichokes
½ cup finely chopped sun-dried tomatoes
⅔ cup finely chopped sun-dried bell
   peppers

CHEESE SAUCE

¼ cup butter
¼ cup all-purpose flour
3 cups whole milk
¾ cup grated gruyère cheese
2 tablespoons chopped basil

Cook the giant shell pasta in a large saucepan of rapidly boiling salted water until *al dente*. Drain and arrange the shells on two non-stick baking sheets to prevent them sticking together. Cover lightly with plastic wrap.

To make the filling, combine all the ingredients in a large bowl. Spoon the filling into the shells, taking care not to overfill them or they will split.

To make the cheese sauce, melt the butter in a small saucepan over low heat. Add the flour and stir for 1 minute, or until golden and smooth. Remove from the heat and gradually stir in the milk. Return to the heat and stir constantly until the sauce boils and begins to thicken. Simmer for a further minute. Remove from the heat and stir in the gruyère cheese with the basil and season to taste.

Preheat the oven to 350°F. Spread 1 cup of the cheese sauce over the base of a 3 quart capacity ovenproof dish. Arrange the filled shell pasta over the sauce, top with the remaining sauce and bake for 30 minutes, or until the sauce is golden.

Pour the bottled pasta sauce in a saucepan and add the oregano. Cook over medium heat for 5 minutes, or until heated through. To serve, divide the sauce among the warmed serving plates, top with the shell pasta and sprinkle with the basil leaves.

Vegetarian Phad Thai

* SERVES 4
* PREPARATION TIME: 20 MINUTES
* COOKING TIME: 5 MINUTES

14 oz flat rice stick noodles
1 small red pepper
3½ oz fried tofu puffs
¼ cup soy sauce
2 tablespoons lime juice
1 tablespoon unpacked brown sugar
2 teaspoons sambal oelek (see Note)
2 tablespoons peanut oil
2 eggs, lightly beaten
1 onion, cut into thin wedges
2 garlic cloves, crushed
6 scallions, thinly sliced on the diagonal
½ cup chopped cilantro leaves
1 cup bean sprouts, trimmed
¼ cup chopped roasted peanuts

Soak the noodles in warm water for 15–20 minutes, or until tender. Drain, then set aside.

Cut the pepper in half, remove the seeds and membrane and cut into thin strips. Cut the fried tofu puffs into ¼ inch wide strips.

To make the stir-fry sauce, combine the soy sauce, lime juice, brown sugar, and sambal oelek in a small bowl.

Heat a wok over high heat. Add enough oil to coat the base and side. Add the egg and swirl to form a thin omelette. Cook for 30 seconds, or until just set. Remove from the wok, roll up, then thinly slice.

Heat the remaining oil in the wok. Add the onion, garlic and pepper and cook over high heat for 2–3 minutes, or until the onion softens. Add the noodles, tossing well. Stir in the slices of omelette, the scallion, tofu, and half of the cilantro. Pour in the stir-fry sauce, then toss to coat the noodles. Sprinkle with the bean sprouts and top with roasted peanuts and the remaining cilantro. Serve immediately.

NOTE: Sambal oelek is a Southeast Asian chili paste.

Cheese-Filled Crepes with Tomato Sauce

❀ MAKES ABOUT 12
❀ PREPARATION TIME: 25 MINUTES
❀ COOKING TIME: 1 HOUR 10 MINUTES

CREPES
1 1/3 cups all-purpose flour
2 cups milk
3 eggs, lightly beaten
1 1/2 tablespoons butter, melted

TOMATO SAUCE
2 tablespoons olive oil
1 garlic clove, crushed
1 2/3 cups canned crushed tomatoes
3 tablespoons chopped Italian parsley

CHEESE FILLING
1 2/3 cups ricotta cheese, crumbled
2/3 cup grated mozzarella cheese
1/4 cup freshly grated parmesan cheese
pinch freshly grated nutmeg
3 tablespoons chopped Italian parsley

1/4 cup freshly grated parmesan cheese,
    extra, to serve
2 tablespoons extra virgin olive oil,
    to drizzle

To make the crepes, sift the flour and 1/2 teaspoon salt into a bowl. Make a well in the center and gradually add the milk, stirring constantly until the mixture is smooth. Add the eggs, little by little, beating well until smooth. Cover and set aside for 30 minutes.

Meanwhile, to make the tomato sauce, heat the oil in a heavy-based frying pan and add the garlic. Cook for 30 seconds over low heat until just golden, then add the tomatoes and 1/2 cup water and season well. Simmer over low heat for 30 minutes, or until the sauce has reduced and thickened. Stir in the parsley.

Heat a crepe pan or non-stick frying pan and brush lightly with the melted butter. Pour 1/4 cup of batter into the pan, swirling quickly to thinly cover the base. Cook for 1 minute, or until the underside is golden. Turn and cook the other side until golden. Transfer to a plate and continue with the remaining batter, stacking the crepes as you go.

Preheat the oven to 400°F and lightly grease a shallow ovenproof dish.

To make the filling, mix all the ingredients together and season well.

To assemble, spread 1 heaped tablespoon of filling over each crepe, leaving a 1/2 inch border. Fold the crepe in half and then in quarters. Place in the ovenproof dish, so that they overlap but are not crowded. Spoon the tomato sauce over the crepes, sprinkle with the extra parmesan and drizzle with the extra virgin olive oil. Bake for 20 minutes, or until heated through.

NOTE: The crepes can be made up to 3 days in advance but must be refrigerated with parchment paper to separate them.

Oriental Mushrooms with Egg Noodles

🌿 SERVES 4

🌿 PREPARATION TIME: 35 MINUTES

🌿 COOKING TIME: 10 MINUTES

9 oz egg noodles
1 red pepper
1 teaspoon sesame oil
1 tablespoon peanut oil
2 garlic cloves, crushed
2 tablespoons grated fresh ginger
6 scallions, sliced
7 oz oyster mushrooms
7 oz shiitake mushrooms, sliced
2 cups snipped garlic chives
¼ cup cashew nuts
2 tablespoons kecap manis (see Note)
¼ cup salt-reduced soy sauce

Soak the hokkein noodles in boiling water for 2 minutes. Drain and set them aside.

Cut the red pepper in half, remove the seeds and membrane and slice.

Heat the oils in a wok and swirl to coat the base and side. Add the garlic, ginger and scallion. Stir-fry over high heat for 2 minutes. Add the red pepper and the oyster and shiitake mushrooms and stir-fry over high heat for 3 minutes, or until the mushrooms are golden.

Stir in the drained noodles. Add the chives, cashews, kecap manis, and soy sauce. Stir-fry for 3 minutes, or until the noodles are coated in the sauce.

NOTE: Kecap manis is an Indonesian sweet soy sauce. If you are unable to find it, use soy sauce sweetened with a little unpacked brown sugar.

Vegetarian Noodles

❀ SERVES 4

❀ PREPARATION TIME: 25 MINUTES

❀ COOKING TIME: 15 MINUTES

½ oz dried shiitake mushrooms
1 cup canned bamboo shoots
½ small red pepper
1 small green pepper
14 oz fresh flat egg noodles
2–3 tablespoons peanut or sunflower oil
1 small carrot, cut into thin batons
¾ cup baby corn, quartered lengthways
1½ cups snow peas, cut into thin batons
1 cup bean sprouts, trimmed
1½ oz wong bok, finely shredded
1 tablespoon thin strips fresh ginger
2 tablespoons vegetable oyster sauce
1 tablespoon mushroom soy sauce
1 tablespoon light soy sauce
1 tablespoon Chinese rice wine
1 teaspoon sesame oil
ground white pepper, to taste
cilantro leaves, to garnish

Cover the mushrooms in boiling water and soak for 20 minutes. Drain. Discard the woody stalks and thinly slice the caps. Drain the bamboo shoots and cut into thin batons. Cut the peppers in half, remove the seeds and membrane, and cut into thin batons.

Cook the noodles in a large saucepan of boiling water for 1 minute, stirring to separate. Drain, rinse under cold running water and drain again.

Heat a wok over high heat, add 1 tablespoon of the oil and swirl to coat the base and side. Stir-fry the carrot and corn for 1–2 minutes, then add the bamboo shoots and stir-fry for a further 1–2 minutes, or until just cooked but still crisp. Remove the vegetables from the wok.

Reheat the wok (add 2 teaspoons peanut oil if necessary) and add the snow peas and red and green pepper. Stir-fry for 1–2 minutes, or until just cooked but still crisp. Add to the carrot and corn mixture. Reheat the wok (add another 2 teaspoons peanut oil if needed), then add the bean sprouts, wong bok and mushrooms and stir-fry for 30 seconds, or until wilted. Add the ginger and stir-fry for a further 1–2 minutes. Remove from the wok and add to the other vegetables.

Heat the remaining oil in the wok, and quickly stir-fry the noodles for 1–2 minutes, or until heated through, taking care not to let them break up. Stir in the oyster sauce, mushroom soy sauce, light soy sauce and rice wine and stir thoroughly. Return all the vegetables to the wok and stir gently for 1–2 minutes, or until well combined with the noodles. Drizzle with the sesame oil, season with white pepper and garnish with the cilantro leaves. Serve immediately.

Baked Eggplants with Tomato and Mozzarella

※ SERVES 6
※ PREPARATION TIME: 20 MINUTES
※ COOKING TIME: 40 MINUTES

6 large slender eggplants, halved
    lengthways, leaving the stems attached
1/2 cup olive oil
2 medium onions, finely chopped
2 medium garlic cloves, crushed
1 2/3 cups canned chopped tomatoes
1 tablespoon concentrated tomato purée
3 tablespoons chopped Italian parsley
1 tablespoon chopped oregano
1 cup grated mozzarella cheese

Preheat the oven to 350°F. Score the eggplant flesh by cutting a criss-cross pattern with a sharp knife, being careful not to cut through the skin. Heat 2 tablespoons of the oil in a large frying pan, add three eggplants and cook for 2–3 minutes each side, or until the flesh is soft. Remove. Repeat with another 2 tablespoons of the oil and the remaining eggplants. Cool slightly and scoop out the flesh, leaving a 1/16 inch border. Finely chop the flesh and reserve the shells.

In the same pan, heat the remaining oil and cook the onion over medium heat for 5 minutes. Add the garlic and cook for 30 seconds, then add the tomato, tomato purée, herbs and eggplant flesh, and cook, stirring occasionally, over low heat for 8–10 minutes, or until the sauce is thick and pulpy. Season well. Arrange the eggplant shells in a lightly greased ovenproof dish and spoon in the tomato filling. Sprinkle with mozzarella and bake for 5–10 minutes, or until the cheese has melted.

Chili Satay Noodles

※ SERVES 4–6
※ PREPARATION TIME: 10 MINUTES
※ COOKING TIME: 10 MINUTES

4 slender eggplants
1 lb 2 oz thin fresh egg noodles
1 tablespoon oil
1 teaspoon sesame oil
1/3 cup peanuts
2 small red chilies
3 cups sugarsnap peas
1 cup trimmed bean sprouts
1/4 cup crunchy peanut butter
1 tablespoon hoisin sauce
1/3 cup coconut milk
2 tablespoons lime juice
1 tablespoon Thai sweet chili sauce

Slice the eggplants. Add the noodles to a large saucepan of boiling water and cook for 3 minutes. Drain, rinse well under cold running water and drain again. Heat the oils in a wok or frying pan. Add the peanuts and toss over high heat for 1 minute, or until golden. Add the chilies, eggplant and sugarsnap peas and cook over high heat for 2 minutes. Reduce the heat to medium and add the noodles and the sprouts. Toss for 1 minute, or until combined.

Blend the peanut butter, hoisin sauce, coconut milk and lime juice until almost smooth. Add to the noodles. Toss over medium heat until the noodles are coated and the sauce is heated.

Baked Eggplant with Tomato and Mozzarella

Braised Vegetables with Cashews

❀ SERVES 4

❀ PREPARATION TIME: 15 MINUTES

❀ COOKING TIME: 10 MINUTES

1 tablespoon peanut oil

2 garlic cloves, crushed

2 teaspoons grated fresh ginger

10½ oz choy sum, cut into 4 inch lengths

¾ cup baby corn, halved lengthways

¾ cup chicken or vegetable stock

¾ cup sliced canned bamboo shoots

5½ oz oyster mushrooms, halved

2 teaspoons cornstarch

2 tablespoons oyster sauce

2 teaspoons sesame oil

1 cup bean sprouts, trimmed

steamed rice, to serve

½ cup unsalted cashew nuts, toasted,
    to serve

Heat a wok over medium heat, add the peanut oil and swirl to coat the base and side. Add the garlic and ginger and stir-fry for 1 minute. Increase the heat to high, add the choy sum and baby corn and stir-fry for another minute.

Add the stock and continue to cook for 3–4 minutes, or until the choy sum stems are just tender. Add the bamboo shoots and mushrooms and cook for 1 minute.

Combine the cornstarch and 1 tablespoon water in a small bowl and mix into a paste. Stir the cornstarch mixture and oyster sauce into the vegetables and cook for 1–2 minutes, or until the sauce is slightly thickened. Stir in the sesame oil and bean sprouts and serve immediately on a bed of steamed rice sprinkled with the toasted cashews.

Harvest Pie

🌿 SERVES 6
🌿 PREPARATION TIME: 40 MINUTES
🌿 COOKING TIME: 1 HOUR

PASTRY

1/2 cup butter, chopped
2 cups all-purpose flour
1/4 cup iced water

FILLING

1 tablespoon olive oil
1 onion, finely chopped
1 small red pepper, seeded, membrane
    removed, and chopped
1 small green pepper, seeded, membrane
    removed, and chopped
5 1/2 oz winter squash, chopped
1 small potato, chopped
3 1/2 oz broccoli, cut into small florets
1 carrot, chopped
1/4 cup butter
1/4 cup all-purpose flour, extra
1 cup milk
2 egg yolks
1/2 cup grated cheddar cheese
1 egg, lightly beaten, to glaze

Preheat the oven to 350°F. To make the pastry, sift the flour into a large bowl. Using your fingertips, rub in the butter until the mixture resembles fine breadcrumbs. Add almost all the water and mix with a flat-bladed knife, using a cutting action until the mixture forms a firm dough, adding more water if necessary. Turn onto a lightly floured work surface and press together until smooth. Divide the dough in half, roll out one portion and line a deep 8 1/4 inch fluted tart pan. Refrigerate for 20 minutes. Roll the remaining pastry out to a 10 inch diameter circle. Cut into strips and lay half of them on a sheet of parchment paper, leaving a 1/2 inch gap between each strip. Interweave the remaining strips to form a lattice pattern. Cover with plastic wrap and refrigerate, keeping flat, until firm.

Cut a sheet of parchment paper to cover the pastry-lined pan. Spread a layer of baking beads or uncooked rice over the paper. Bake for 10 minutes, remove from the oven and discard the paper and beads. Bake for another 10 minutes, or until lightly golden. Allow to cool.

To make the filling, heat the oil in a frying pan. Add the onion and cook for 2 minutes, or until soft. Add the pepper and cook, stirring, for 3 minutes. Steam or boil the remaining vegetables until just tender. Drain and cool. Mix the onion, pepper and other vegetables in a large bowl. Heat the butter in a small saucepan. Add the flour and cook, stirring, for 2 minutes. Add the milk and stir constantly over medium heat until the mixture boils and thickens. Boil for 1 minute and then remove from the heat. Add the egg yolks and cheese and stir until smooth. Pour the sauce over the vegetables and stir to combine. Pour the mixture into the pastry case and brush the edges with the egg. Using the parchment paper to lift, invert the pastry lattice over the vegetables. Remove the paper, trim the pastry edges and brush with the egg, sealing it to the cooked pastry. Brush the top with egg and bake for 30 minutes, or until golden brown.

Sweet Vegetable Curry

※ SERVES 4
※ PREPARATION TIME: 20 MINUTES
※ COOKING TIME: 40 MINUTES

2 carrots
1 parsnip
1 potato
1 green pepper
2 tablespoons oil
2 onions, chopped
1 teaspoon ground cardamom
$1/4$ teaspoon ground cloves
$1^1/2$ teaspoons cumin seeds
1 teaspoon ground coriander
1 teaspoon ground turmeric
1 teaspoon brown mustard seeds
$1/2$ teaspoon chili powder
2 teaspoons grated fresh ginger
$1^1/3$ cups vegetable stock
$3/4$ cup apricot nectar
2 tablespoons fruit chutney
7 oz small white mushrooms
$10^1/2$ oz cauliflower, cut into small florets
$1/4$ cup ground almonds

Cut the carrots, parsnip and potato into $3/4$ inch pieces. Cut the pepper in half, remove the seeds and membrane and cut into $3/4$ inch squares.

Heat the oil in a large heavy-based saucepan. Add the onion and cook over medium heat for 4 minutes, or until just soft. Add the cardamom, cloves, cumin seeds, ground coriander, turmeric, mustard seeds, chili powder, and ginger and cook, stirring, for 1 minute or until aromatic.

Add the carrot, parsnip, potato, vegetable stock, apricot nectar and fruit chutney to the pan. Cook, covered, over medium heat for 25 minutes, stirring occasionally.

Stir in the pepper, mushrooms, and cauliflower. Simmer for 10 minutes, or until the vegetables are tender. Stir in the ground almonds and serve with rice.

NOTE: Any vegetables can be used in this curry. For example, broccoli, zucchini, red pepper or sweet potato would also be suitable.

Mushroom Nut Roast with Tomato Sauce

☙ SERVES 6

☙ PREPARATION TIME: 30 MINUTES

☙ COOKING TIME: 1 HOUR

1 large onion
10½ oz mushrooms
2 tablespoons olive oil
2 medium garlic cloves, crushed
¼ cup cashew nuts
¼ cup brazil nuts
1 cup grated cheddar cheese
¼ cup freshly grated parmesan cheese
1 egg, lightly beaten
2 tablespoons snipped chives
1 cup fresh whole-wheat breadcrumbs
chives, extra, to garnish

TOMATO SAUCE
1 medium onion
1½ tablespoons olive oil
1 medium garlic clove, crushed
14 oz canned chopped tomatoes
1 tablespoon concentrated tomato purée
1 teaspoon sugar

Grease a 5½ x 8¼ inch bar pan and line the base with parchment paper.

Dice the onion and finely chop the mushrooms. Heat the oil in a frying pan and add the onion, garlic and mushrooms. Fry until soft, then cool.

Process the nuts in a food processor until finely chopped, but do not overprocess. Preheat the oven to 350°F.

Combine the cooled mushroom mixture, chopped nuts, cheddar, parmesan, egg, chives and breadcrumbs in a bowl. Mix well and season to taste. Press into the bar pan and bake for 45 minutes, or until firm. Leave for 5 minutes, then turn out and garnish with the extra chives. Cut into slices to serve.

Meanwhile, to make the tomato sauce, finely chop the onion. Heat the oil in a saucepan, add the onion and garlic and cook, stirring frequently, for 5 minutes, or until soft but not brown. Stir in the tomato, concentrated tomato purée, sugar and ⅓ cup water. Simmer gently for 3–5 minutes, or until slightly thickened. Season. Serve the tomato sauce with the sliced nut roast.

NOTE: For a variation, use a different mixture of nuts and add some seeds. You can use nuts such as pecans, almonds, hazelnuts (without skins) and pine nuts. Suitable seeds to use include sesame, pumpkin or sunflower seeds.

Potato Noodles with Vegetables

☙ SERVES 4
☙ PREPARATION TIME: 25 MINUTES
☙ COOKING TIME: 25 MINUTES

4 scallions
2 carrots
1 lb 2 oz baby pak choy (or 9 oz spinach)
10½ oz dried potato starch noodles
   (see Notes)
⅓ cup black fungus (see Notes)
¼ cup sesame oil
2 tablespoons vegetable oil
3 garlic cloves, finely chopped
1½ inch piece fresh ginger, grated
¼ cup shoyu (Japanese soy sauce)
   (see Notes)
2 tablespoons mirin
1 teaspoon sugar
2 tablespoons sesame and seaweed sprinkle
   (see Notes)

Finely chop two of the scallions. Slice the remaining scallions into 1½ inch pieces. Cut the carrots into 1½ inch batons. Roughly chop the baby pak choy.

Cook the noodles in a large saucepan of boiling water for about 5 minutes, or until they are translucent. Drain and rinse thoroughly under cold running water until the noodles are cold (this will also remove any excess starch). Use scissors to roughly chop the noodles into shorter lengths (this will make them easier to eat with chopsticks).

Pour hot water over the black fungus and soak for about 10 minutes.

Heat 1 tablespoon of the sesame oil with the vegetable oil in a large heavy-based frying pan or wok. Cook the garlic, ginger, and finely chopped scallion for 3 minutes over medium heat, stirring regularly. Add the carrot and stir-fry for 1 minute. Add the drained cooled noodles, sliced scallion, pak choy, remaining sesame oil, the soy sauce, mirin, and sugar. Toss well to coat the noodles with the sauce. Cover and cook over low heat for 2 minutes. Add the drained fungus, then cover and cook for 2 minutes. Scatter over the sesame and seaweed sprinkle and serve immediately.

NOTES : Potato starch noodles are also known as Korean pasta and are available from Asian food stores.
   Dried black fungus, shoyu (Japanese soy sauce) and sesame and seaweed sprinkle are all available from Asian food stores.

Minestrone Soup with Rice

1 cup dried cranberry beans
¼ cup butter
1 onion, finely chopped
1 garlic clove, finely chopped
3 tablespoons finely chopped Italian
   parsley
2 sage leaves
3½ oz pancetta, cubed
2 celery stalks, halved, then sliced
2 carrots, sliced
3 potatoes, peeled
1 teaspoon concentrated tomato purée
1⅔ cups canned chopped tomatoes
8 basil leaves
12 cups chicken or vegetable stock
2 zucchinis, sliced
1½ cups fresh peas
4½ oz green beans, cut into 1½ inch
   lengths
¼ cabbage, shredded
1 cup risotto rice
freshly grated parmesan cheese, to serve

Put the dried beans in a large bowl, cover with cold water, and soak overnight. Drain and rinse under cold water.

Melt the butter in a saucepan and add the onion, garlic, parsley, sage, and pancetta. Cook over low heat, stirring once or twice, for 10 minutes, or until the onion is softened but not browned. Add the celery, carrot, and potatoes, and cook for 5 minutes. Stir in the tomato purée, tomatoes, basil, and borlotti beans. Season with freshly ground black pepper. Pour in the stock and bring slowly to a boil. Cover and leave to simmer for 2 hours, stirring once or twice.

If the potatoes have not broken up by the end of the 2 hours, roughly break them with a fork against the side of the pan. Season to taste then add the zucchini, peas, green beans, cabbage, and rice. Simmer for a further 15–20 minutes, or until the rice is cooked. Divide among six soup bowls and sprinkle with a little parmesan cheese, to serve.

Tortellini with Eggplant

* SERVES 4
* PREPARATION TIME: 10 MINUTES
* COOKING TIME: 20 MINUTES

1 red pepper
1 lb 2 oz eggplant
1 lb 2 oz fresh cheese and spinach
    tortellini
1/4 cup vegetable oil
2 garlic cloves, crushed
1 3/4 cups canned crushed tomatoes
1 cup vegetable stock
1/2 cup chopped basil

Cut the pepper in half, remove the seeds and membrane, and cut into small squares. Cut the eggplant into small cubes.

Cook the tortellini in a large saucepan of rapidly boiling salted water until *al dente*. Drain and return to the pan.

While the pasta is cooking, heat the oil in a large frying pan, add the garlic and red pepper, and stir over medium heat for 1 minute. Add the eggplant to the pan and stir gently over medium heat for 5 minutes, or until lightly browned.

Add the tomatoes and vegetable stock to the pan. Stir and bring to a boil. Reduce the heat to low, cover the pan, and cook for 10 minutes, or until the vegetables are tender. Add the basil and pasta and stir until mixed through.

NOTE: Cut the eggplant just before using, as it turns brown when exposed to the air.

Green Curry with Sweet Potato and Eggplant

❀ SERVES 4–6

❀ PREPARATION TIME: 15 MINUTES

❀ COOKING TIME: 25 MINUTES

1 eggplant

1 tablespoon vegetable oil

1 onion, chopped

1–2 tablespoons green curry paste
   (see Note)

1½ cups coconut milk

1 cup vegetable stock

6 kaffir lime leaves

1 sweet potato, cut into cubes

2 teaspoons grated jaggery or soft
   brown sugar

2 tablespoons lime juice

2 teaspoons lime zest

cilantro leaves, to garnish

kaffir lime leaves, extra, to garnish
   (optional)

steamed rice, to serve

Chop the onion. Quarter and slice the eggplant. Heat the oil in a large wok. Add the onion and green curry paste and cook, stirring, over medium heat for 3 minutes. Add the eggplant and cook for a further 4–5 minutes, or until softened. Pour in the coconut milk and vegetable stock, bring to a boil, then reduce the heat and simmer for 5 minutes. Add the kaffir lime leaves and sweet potato and cook, stirring occasionally, for 10 minutes, or until the eggplant and sweet potato are very tender.

Mix in the jaggery, lime juice, and lime zest until well combined with the vegetables. Season to taste with salt. Garnish with some cilantro leaves and extra kaffir lime leaves if desired, and serve with steamed rice.

NOTE: Make sure you read the label and choose a green curry paste without shrimp paste.

Hungarian Casserole

☙ SERVES 4–6

☙ PREPARATION TIME: 30 MINUTES

☙ COOKING TIME: 30 MINUTES

1 red pepper

1 green pepper

1 tablespoon olive oil

1½ tablespoons butter

1 onion, chopped

4 large potatoes, cut into chunks

1¾ cups canned chopped tomatoes

1 cup vegetable stock

2 teaspoons caraway seeds

2 teaspoons paprika

CRISPY CROUTONS

4 slices white bread

1 cup vegetable oil

Cut the red and green peppers in half, remove the seeds and membrane, and roughly chop. Heat the oil and butter in a large heavy-based frying pan and cook the potato over medium heat, turning regularly, until crisp on the edges.

Add the onion and red and green pepper and cook for 5 minutes. Add the tomatoes, vegetable stock, caraway seeds and paprika. Season to taste. Simmer, uncovered, for 10 minutes or until the potatoes are tender.

Meanwhile, to make the croutons, remove the crusts from the bread and cut the bread into small cubes. Heat the oil in a frying pan over medium heat. Cook the bread, turning often, for 2 minutes or until golden brown and crisp. Drain on paper towels. Serve the croutons with the casserole.

Tofu and Snow Pea Stir-Fry

☙ SERVES 4

☙ PREPARATION TIME: 10 MINUTES

☙ COOKING TIME: 15 MINUTES

1 lb 5 oz firm tofu, drained

¼ cup peanut oil

2 teaspoons sambal oelek or chili paste
   (see Notes)

2 garlic cloves, finely chopped

10½ oz snow peas, trimmed

14 oz fresh Asian mushrooms (such as
   shiitake or oyster), sliced

¼ cup kecap manis (see Notes)

Cut the tofu into ¾ inch cubes. Heat a wok over high heat, add 2 tablespoons of the peanut oil and swirl to coat the base and side of the wok. Add the tofu in two batches and stir-fry each batch for 2–3 minutes, or until lightly browned on all sides, then transfer to a plate. Heat the remaining oil in the wok, add the sambal oelek, garlic, snow peas, mushrooms, and 1 tablespoon water and stir-fry for 1–2 minutes, or until the vegetables are almost cooked but still crunchy. Return the tofu to the wok, add the kecap manis and stir-fry for 1 minute, or until heated through. Serve immediately with steamed rice.

NOTES: Sambal oelek is a Southeast Asian chili paste.
   Kecap manis is an Indonesian sweet soy sauce. If you are unable to find it, use soy sauce sweetened with a little unpacked brown sugar.

Hungarian Casserole

Spinach and Ricotta Cannelloni

※ SERVES 6
※ PREPARATION TIME: 1 HOUR
※ COOKING TIME: 1 HOUR 15 MINUTES

1 large onion
20 cups firmly packed spinach
13 oz fresh lasagne sheets
2 tablespoons olive oil
1–2 medium garlic cloves, crushed
2 1/3 cups beaten ricotta cheese
2 eggs, beaten
1/4 teaspoon freshly grated nutmeg

TOMATO SAUCE
1 medium onion
1 lb 2 oz very ripe medium tomatoes
1 tablespoon olive oil
2 medium garlic cloves, finely chopped
2 tablespoons concentrated tomato purée
1 teaspoon unpacked brown sugar
1 cup grated mozzarella cheese

Finely chop the onion and spinach. Cut the lasagne sheets into 15 even-sized pieces and trim lengthways so that they will fit neatly into a deep-sided, rectangular ovenproof dish when filled. Bring a large saucepan of water to a rapid boil and cook 1–2 lasagne sheets at a time until just softened. The amount of time will differ, depending on the type and brand of lasagne, but is usually about 2 minutes. Remove the sheets carefully with a wide strainer or sieve and lay out flat on a clean, damp dish towel. Return the water to a boil and repeat the process with the remaining pasta sheets.

Heat the oil in a heavy-based frying pan. Cook the onion and garlic until golden, stirring regularly. Add the washed spinach, cook for 2 minutes, cover with a tight-fitting lid and steam for 5 minutes. Drain, removing as much liquid as possible. The spinach must be quite dry or the pasta will be soggy. Combine the spinach with the ricotta, eggs and nutmeg, and season to taste. Mix well and set aside.

To make the tomato sauce, chop the onion and tomatoes. Heat the oil in a frying pan and cook the onion and garlic for 10 minutes over low heat, stirring occasionally. Add the tomato including the juice, the concentrated tomato purée, sugar, 1/2 cup water and season. Bring the sauce to a boil, reduce the heat and simmer for 10 minutes.

Preheat the oven to 350°F. Lightly brush the ovenproof dish with melted butter or oil. Spread about one-third of the tomato sauce over the base of the dish. Working with one piece of lasagne at a time, spoon 2 1/2 tablespoons of the spinach mixture down the center of the sheet, leaving a border at each end. Roll up and place, seam side down, in the dish. Repeat with the remaining pasta and filling. Spoon the remaining tomato sauce over the cannelloni and scatter the mozzarella over the top. Bake for 30–35 minutes, or until golden brown and bubbling. Set aside for 10 minutes before serving. Garnish with fresh herb sprigs if desired.

Tofu in Black Bean Sauce

⚘ SERVES 4

⚘ PREPARATION TIME: 20 MINUTES

⚘ COOKING TIME: 15 MINUTES

1 red pepper

1 lb firm tofu

10^1/$_2$ oz baby pak choy

^{1}/$_4$ cup canned black beans, rinsed and
    drained

4 scallions

^{1}/$_3$ cup vegetable stock

2 teaspoons cornstarch

2 teaspoons Chinese rice wine

1 teaspoon sesame oil

1 tablespoon soy sauce

2 tablespoons peanut oil

2 garlic cloves, very finely chopped

2 teaspoons finely chopped fresh ginger

steamed rice, to serve

Cut the red pepper in half, remove the seeds and membrane, and cut into ^{3}/$_4$ inch chunks. Cut the tofu into^3/$_4$ inch cubes and chop the baby pak choy, crossways, into ^{3}/$_4$ inch pieces. Finely chop the black beans and slice the scallions, diagonally, including some green.

Combine the vegetable stock, cornstarch, Chinese rice wine, sesame oil, soy sauce, ^{1}/$_2$ teaspoon salt, and some freshly ground black pepper.

Heat a wok over medium heat, add the peanut oil and swirl to coat the base and side. Add the tofu and stir-fry in two batches for 3 minutes each batch, or until lightly browned. Remove with a slotted spoon and drain on paper towels. Discard any bits of tofu stuck to the wok or floating in the oil.

Add the garlic and ginger and stir-fry for 30 seconds. Toss in the black beans and scallion and stir-fry for 30 seconds. Add the pepper and stir-fry for 1 minute. Add the pak choy and stir-fry for 2 minutes. Return the tofu to the wok and stir gently. Pour in the sauce and stir gently for 2–3 minutes, or until the sauce has thickened slightly. Serve immediately with steamed rice.

index

Published in 2009 by Murdoch Books Pty Limited

Murdoch Books Australia
Pier 8/9
23 Hickson Road
Millers Point NSW 2000
Phone: +61 (0) 2 8220 2000
Fax: +61 (0) 2 8220 2558
www.murdochbooks.com.au

Murdoch Books UK Limited
Erico House, 6th Floor
93–99 Upper Richmond Road
Putney, London SW15 2TG
Phone: +44 (0) 20 8785 5995
Fax: +44 (0) 20 8785 5985
www.murdochbooks.co.uk

Chief Executive: Juliet Rogers
Publishing Director: Kay Scarlett

Design concept: Heather Menzies
Design layout: Sarah Odgers
Photographer: Jared Fowler
Stylist: Cherise Koch
Production: Alexandra Gonzalez

ISBN 978 1 74196 163 8

Colour separation by Splitting Image
Printed by Imago in 2009. PRINTED IN MALAYSIA.

IMPORTANT: Those who might be at risk from the effects of salmonella poisoning (the elderly, pregnant women, young children and those suffering from immune deficiency diseases) should consult their doctor with any concerns about eating raw eggs.

OVEN GUIDE: You may find cooking times vary depending on the oven you are using. For fan-forced ovens, as a general rule, set the oven temperature to 20°C (35°F) lower than indicated in the recipe.